Plant It Now, Dry It Later

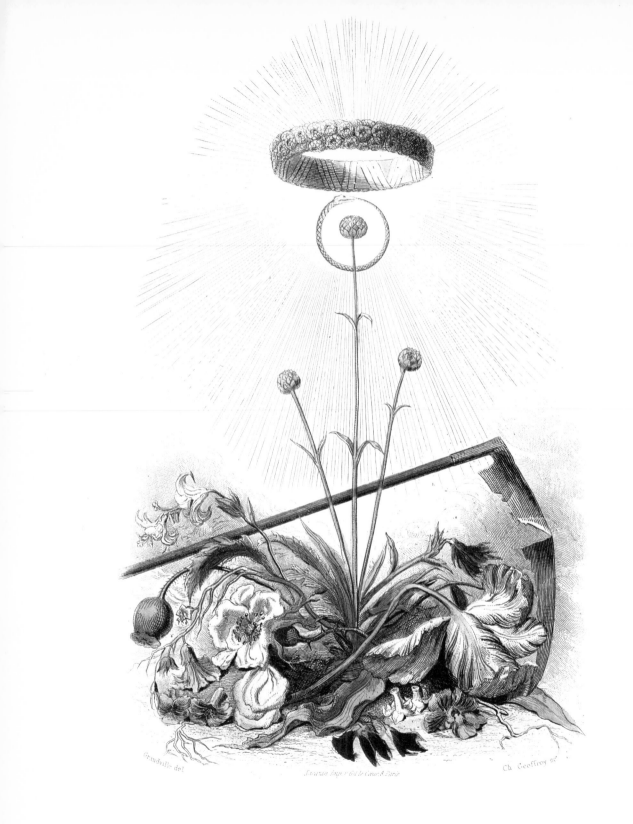

IMMORTELLE

Plant It Now, Dry It Later

Harriet Floyd

McGraw-Hill Book Company
New York   St. Louis   San Francisco
Düsseldorf   Mexico   Sydney   Toronto

CREDITS:

The botanical prints were photographed through the courtesy of The New York Botanical Garden.

Claude Monet's *Sunflowers,* courtesy of the Metropolitan Museum of Art. Bequest of Mrs. H. O. Havemeyer, 1929. The H. O. Havemeyer Collection.

Jan Brueghel's *Flowers in a Blue Vase,* courtesy of Kunsthistorisches Museum and Photo Meyer K. G., Vienna, Austria.

All photographs by Harriet Floyd.

Figure 14 created by Beverly Bailey.

Book Design, Elaine Gongora

First Edition

123456789 BP BP 79876543

Library of Congress Cataloging in Publication Data

Floyd, Harriet.
    Plant it now, dry it later.
    1. Dried flower arrangement. 2. Flowers—Drying.
3. Flower gardening. 4. Flowers. I. Title.
SB449.3.D7F5   745.92   73-4260
ISBN 0-07-021387-9

Acknowledgments

In undertaking *Plant It Now, Dry It Later* I have drawn upon the knowledge and talents of many delightful people, and to them I wish to express my deepest gratitude. The enthusiastic horticultural efforts and generosity of many gardening friends, particularly Louise Lamalle, Beverly Bailey, Gertrude Schweikhardt, and Anna Williams, enabled me to experiment with, and include here, many flowers that do not grow in my own garden. Their joy of flowers gives testimony to the old Chinese proverb ". . . if you want to be happy forever, be a gardener."

Much of the research for *Plant It Now, Dry It Later,* other than the actual experimenting with the flowers, was accomplished in the library at the New York Botanical Garden which houses the largest collection of botanical literature in the Western Hemisphere. Every request for assistance, however large or small, was met with enthusiasm by Mr. Frank J. Anderson, Assistant to the Librarian, Mrs. Lothian Lynas, Assistant Librarian, and Mrs. Sonia Wedge, Reference Librarian.

My acquaintance with the Garden extended beyond the library when a request for assistance in the identification of several flowers was met by Dr. Howard S. Irwin, President of the New York Botanical Garden. Dr. Irwin was, at that time, Head Curator of The Herbarium, one of the world's great plant specimen museums. The Herbarium contains more than 4,000,000 pressed specimens of the earth's flora, which have been carefully catalogued and are closeted in a thousand steel cabinets. These specimens are a storehouse of plant information and are shared with ecologists and plant scientists the world over. As *Plant It Now, Dry It Later* progressed, I invited Dr. Irwin to read the manuscript and his many suggestions contributed greatly to its botanical accuracy. Mr. Dennis Brown, Director of Horticulture at the New York Botanical Garden, graciously assisted in the identification of the flowers which Jan Brueghel included in his painting *Flowers in a Blue Vase.*

The same helpfulness and interest that I experienced in the library of the New York Botanical Garden also prevails in the library of the Botany Department in the Natural History Museum in London, where I spent several days browsing through some of the largest and heaviest tomes I have ever seen. It is not surprising that the great beauty contained in these rarely opened, mostly nineteenth-century, volumes has remained virtually unappreciated through the years, for a strong back is required to lift them from their shelves!

The butterflies which grace several of the arrangements are from the collection of John J. Bowe, M.D., whose enthusiasm as a lepidopterist is exceeded only by his skill as a plastic surgeon.

The gentle encouragement and patience of my husband, William Hurd Floyd, M.D., and my son, Robert Vincent Floyd, who shared the experience of living in my ever expanding dry garden, must be noted with deep appreciation.

Finally, regardless of the amount of time one devotes to experimenting and research, a project such as this is never completed until the last page has been typed—an accomplishment achieved through the dedicated efforts of Phyllis Kobiash and Harriet Stover.

To all I am grateful.

Harriet Floyd

Contents

Flowers, Flowers, Flowers!

In all of nature nothing has contributed more to our sense of beauty, color, and design than flowers, and the desire to capture their transient beauty has occupied man since ancient times.

The pleasures of planning a garden and reaping the harvest are almost as old as mankind. As the vegetable garden delights the palate, so the flower garden delights the eye; and, as we preserve the bounty of the vegetable garden to nourish the body, should we not also preserve our flowers to nourish the soul?

Plant It Now, Dry It Later is devoted to preserving the colorful flowers of the garden. With but few exceptions I have left the nuts and pods and other brown materials that usually come to mind when "dried flowers" are mentioned for others to write about, for my spirit finds joy in the color that late autumn plant materials cannot equal.

The joy of color and the joy of flowers are not new. Man has reveled in both since time began and in every age he has sought to surround himself with their beauty. One can imagine the thrill which must have surged through the soul of our early Mediterranean ancestor as the earth beneath his feet became a carpet of the bright reds and blues of Anemone interlaced with yellow and white Crocus; and before he learned to use its stamen and its style to make a yellow dye for cloth how eagerly he must have picked the Crocus, hoping to capture its beauty, only to have it fade moments later in his hands!

Some of the flowers he picked did not fade so quickly

Crocus (P. J. Redouté)

as others, and as names were gradually assigned to plants these were called Amaranthus, which in Greek means "does not wither or wax old," and distinguishes the Everlasting flowers such as Globe Amaranth and Cockscomb from the more perishable blossoms such as the Anemone and Crocus.

If many of the flowers were fleeting, man was persistent in his efforts to capture their beauty, and, as he found that he could not preserve the real flowers, he turned to the more permanent materials about him—the stone and the bronze, the tiles and the pottery—and on these he carved and traced the likenesses of their forms.

China, whose ancient name *Hua* can be translated as *flower*, has been called the Mother of Gardens because so many of her beautiful native flowering plants adapt themselves so readily to garden planting. There is hardly a garden in the North Temperate Zone that does not flaunt some of China's floral beauty—the Rhododendrons, Peonies, China Asters, Roses, Primroses, and Chrysanthemums, to name but a very few. It is not suprising, then, that thousands of years ago, long before man began to record the history of events, the people of Hua were recording their joy and love of the beautiful flowers all about them as they decorated their cooking utensils, mirror fittings, and small personal ornaments with floral designs.

As history (and plants?) moved westward Queen Hatshepsut's gardeners transplanted trees from gardens in the land of Punt (a country believed situated along the southern shore of the Red Sea) to the gardens of Egypt, and their efforts were recorded as an historical event in her temple at Deir el Bahri. The trees in Queen Hatshepsut's gardens have long since been lost in the sands of time, but their beauty and that of the fluffy yellow flowers of the Acacia, often captured by these same Egyptian stone carvers in colored bas-relief to adorn the poolsides of the wealthy, have long survived their ancient artisans.

As the stone carvers recorded the beauty of flowers they sometimes captured their political significance. Twenty-five hundred years ago the Lotus symbolized Upper Egypt, and

China Aster (P. J. Redouté)

the Papyrus, Lower Egypt. When Rameses II united the two nations, their political union was recorded for posterity by the carvers who knotted forever in stone the stems of the two plants at the entrance to Rameses' Great Temple at Abu Simbel in Upper Egypt.

Other plants and flowers have played important roles in the history of nations. In Ireland, in 432, the Christian missionary Patrick is said to have used the Shamrock to illustrate the Holy Trinity with such effectiveness that many pagans were converted to Christianity and the Shamrock became the national emblem.

The three petals of the Iris symbolized faith, wisdom, and valor, and represented power to Egyptian rulers of long ago. This political interpretation so captivated the Capetian king and Crusader, Louis VII, in 1147 that he adopted the Iris as the emblem of his house. It became known as the "Fleur de Louis" or "Flower of Louis," which was corrupted to its present Fleur de Lis.

Iris (P. J. Redouté)

The Tulip, a flower of great popularity in Turkey, was chosen as the emblem of the ruling house of Osman, and the Chrysanthemum was correspondingly honored in Japan.

The political significance of flowers has diminished in our age and our political emotions are less likely to be aroused by a floral emblem than were the political emotions of our ancestors. For centuries the Thistle evoked visions of the mighty kilted Scotsmen, and the Fleur-de-Lis, the royalty of France, but I suspect that the political fires these flowers once fanned have been banked by the dampers of time.

In the United States we have our state flowers: New Jersey has its Violet, Connecticut its Mountain Laurel, and California its Poppy; New York, Iowa, and North Dakota honor the Rose, but in none of these states does the Rose evoke the fervor that the white Rose of York and the red Rose of Lancaster evoked among the English princes during the War of the Roses in the middle of the fifteenth century.

The significance of flowers, whether political, religious, or romantic, is virtually endless. "The Turks," wrote John

Rose (P. J. Redouté)

Parkinson in 1640, "will not suffer a Rose leafe to lye upon the ground, or any to tread on them in honor of their Mahomet, from whose sweat they are persuaded the Rose sprang up." Buddhists, Taoists, and Christians all adorn their altars with floral offerings to their Gods, and today's bride is as eager to carry the traditional bouquet or to wear flowers in her hair on her wedding day as was the bride of ancient Greece.

The Madonna Lily, so popular in Christian churches at Eastertime, currently elicits religious emotions of the resurrection of Christ, but during the Middle Ages the Lily symbolized virginity, innocence, and purity, and artists of the period were exhorted by the Church to include this lovely white flower in their paintings of the Annunciation. We express our joy and our grief, our love, admiration, and appreciation as we say with flowers what Wordsworth said that only flowers could express: "Thoughts that do often lie too deep for tears."

Man's expressions of his joy in flowers have created decorative beauty through the ages, but needless to say these are only substitutes for God's own creations, for no medium, whether it is stone, wood, or paint, can capture the true beauty of real flowers in all of their glorious variations of color, form, and detail.

Plant It Now, Dry It Later Flowers

All of the *Plant It Now, Dry It Later* flowers, which includes fruits and seeds, and foliage recommended for use in the dried bouquet, grow in the three *Plant It Now, Dry It Later* gardens:

Your Own Garden
The Local Florist Garden
Everyone's Roadside Garden: Pick With Care!

I have classified the flowers, regardless of the gardens in which they grow, according to the simple techniques by which they are dried (an accommodation to the motivation of the gardener/flower dryer/arranger, and/or the climate in which he may live):

1. The Lazy Flowers. These are the everlasting kinds of flowers such as Strawflower, Immortelle, and Statice that continue to bloom long after the growing season has ended.

2. The More Effort Flowers. The Tulip, Rose, Anemone, and Lily are but a very few of our garden flowers that pass into oblivion at the end of the growing season. I refer to these as the More Effort Flowers for now, with just a *little* more effort than is required to dry the Lazy Flowers (which is virtually no effort at all), it is possible to capture their colorful, three-dimensional beauty!

While browsing through the book and print stalls along the Left Bank of the Seine in Paris I spied the print *Immortelle*, Fig. 1, which portrayed the two classifications of *Plant It Now, Dry It Later* flowers so vividly that I wondered,

Immortelle (Figure 1)

perchance, if our meeting were more than pure coincidence? Could it be that its creator, the whimsical French flower illustrator, Grandville, had anticipated the arrival of *Plant It Now, Dry It Later* some 120 years later?

A flight of fancy, of course, but Grandville must have been captivated by the two kinds of garden flowers. He illustrated their differences in the golden *Immortelle,* a popular French everlasting flower, blooming above the faded Tulip, Anemone, Lily and other flowers that fade and die when the garden harvest has ended.

THE LAZY FLOWERS.

An arrangement of Lazy Flowers

In addition to Everlastings, the Lazy Flowers include flowers such as Pussy Willow and Erica, and fruits such as Bittersweet and Honesty, all of which, when picked at the proper time and dried in the medium of air, will share their decorative beauty with you indoors for many months or even years.

People everywhere have recognized the decorative beauty of their Lazy Flowers. The Australians have their Acroclinium, Rhodanthe, and Strawflower, which is one of the most popular motifs in Australian decorative design. The East Indians have their Globe Amaranth and Cockscomb, and for centuries East Indian women have woven gay tiaras and garlands of Globe Amaranth to wear in their hair and to decorate musical instruments at festival times.

In Germany, in midsummer, when the fields are perfumed with the sweet fragrance of Erica, women weave handled baskets of the colorful flowered spikes, then fill them with more Erica to give as charming and lasting gifts.

The eighteenth-century housewife in Williamsburg, Virginia, decorated her home in winter with our Lazy Flowers, and recreations of these charming Colonial bouquets are among the most popular winter floral decorations today.

The Lazy Flowers cater to two groups of people. The first includes those who say, "I'd love to have some dried arrangements, but I'm not a great gardener and I don't want to fuss with all the wiring and the sand or whatever you use." Many charming arrangements can be created with the Lazy Flowers; they are easy to plant, easy to grow, and simple to dry. Few require wiring. They are less susceptible to the vagaries of the weather and will provide endless pleasure long after the summer garden has faded into memory, and I recommend them heartily to the modest gardener or arranger.

The second group for whom the Lazy Flowers are especially useful are those who live, as I do, in areas where summer humidity often soars above seventy percent. Bitter is the disappointment of the flower dryer who successfully dries some bright garden treasures in sand or silica gel and stores them for another day only to find that dampness has turned them into brown disappointment.

Unless you have some reasonable control over high summer humidity, either by air conditioning or a dehumidification system, it would be well for you to concentrate your gardening and drying efforts on the Lazy Flowers. But try some of the More Effort Flowers, too: those that bloom in the spring and can be arranged under glass before the summer humidity arrives, or those that flower later in the growing season and in the local florist garden throughout the winter. Success with the early- and later-blooming flowers processed in silica gel can be a bonus, but failure will not leave you with a dearth of colorful materials for winter decoration. (See "Storing," page 97.)

THE MORE EFFORT FLOWERS

For years I have been intrigued with the idea of preserving some of this garden beauty for winter decoration when the garden is dormant and fresh flowers are expensive. Imagine being able to pick real flowers such as the Crocus, Peony, and Rose that never stop blooming in a garden that knows no season! The decorative possibilities become almost endless.

Now, through the use of a few simple techniques and a desiccating medium called silica gel, my Daffodils bloom

Peonies bloom in November

in January. An advance on the growing season? No mention that they bloomed in last year's garden! Zinnias and Marigolds in February? A friend with a greenhouse, perhaps? Tulips and Peonies in November? Are they plastic or silk? They look real! They *are* real, of course, and with just a little more effort than it takes to dry the Lazy Flowers you can preserve much of the transient beauty of your garden to enjoy at every season of the year.

Collecting the many More Effort Flowers has taken me into more gardens than I care to admit, and I am more than grateful to my enthusiastic gardening friends whose efforts provided much of the floral variety discussed and illustrated in this book. Several years of experiment developed techniques that retain the fresh, natural forms of the flowers during processing and determined the time required to dry each one in silica gel.

With the exception of the Iris, which becomes extremely fragile when dry, I have omitted flowers that require special handling and have included only those which will provide maximum pleasure commensurate with the motivation and interest of the hobbyist. If "how-to" projects become too tedious they are not fun and the pleasures they should provide are lost in the frustrations of impatience and failure.

All of the flowers, fruits, seeds, and foliage discussed here can be processed sucessfully if the simple directions are followed. Most important is the careful attention to the stage of development of the flower when it is picked for processing. (See "Timing," page 79.)

About Gardens and Plants

Much of the romance of gardens and plants seems to have been lost in the last generation or two. We are inclined to accept our gardens as if they have always been with us, but, in fact, it was not really so many years ago—about the time that Christopher Columbus was turning the eyes of Europe to the Western world—that almost all the plants that grew in Europe were in the fields and meadows, along the streams, and in the woodlands. God's Garden was everywhere and man's garden was virtually nowhere.

And there were not nearly so many sorts of plants in God's European garden then as there are in man's European garden now. The Tulip would not arrive in Vienna from Constantinople until 1562, and the Baby's-Breath still resided in the fields about St. Petersburg. The Dahlia had not left its home in the cool Mexican hills, and the Freesia was known only to its neighbors in distant South Africa. The Tree Peony had yet to learn of the Occidental World; the Iceland Poppy lived under the rule of the Czars. All of this garden beauty we accept so readily as our own and as our European floral heritage when, in truth, our American garden is an international floral melting pot!

Although man has responded to the beauty and color of flowers since time began, plants have not always been appreciated for their beauty alone. In 1633 John Gerard

Tree Peony

Gerard's "true-blacke Hellebor" *(Helleborus niger)*

explained in "To the Reader" of his *Herball*[1] "That God of his infinite goodness and bountie hath by the medium of Plants, bestowed almost all food, clothing, and medicine upon man." Agriculture, the growing of plants for food and fiber, had been known for thousands of years, and ancient Greek and Egyptian physicians had employed certain plants for their medicinal virtues in the treatment of patients. The root of Christmas Rose *(Helleborus niger),* for example, was considered useful in the treatment of epilepsy and arthritis. It is not surprising, then, that the first garden in Europe, established by Luca Ghini in Pisa in 1543, cultivated plants not for their visible beauty but, rather, for their medicinal virtues, which were studied by the medical students of the sixteenth century. Latin was the scientific language of the day and Luca Ghini's garden was called a *hortus medicus*—literally, a *medical garden.*

The mind of man being what it is, where there was one garden it was followed by others, and a *hortus medicus* sprang up at Padua, at Florence, at Rome and Bologna; they spread northward to Amsterdam, Leyden, and Uppsala.

As the Renaissance flourished and commerce and wealth

---

[1] Herbals were the home medical books of the fifteenth to seventeenth centuries, and Gerard's *Herball, or Generall Historie of Plantes* contains descriptions and woodcuts of each plant and discusses their virtues, medicinal and otherwise. For instance, his index on the "Virtues of Plants" includes such items as "To cure the Lunaticke," "A medicine against Madness," "To preserve grapes a whole year," "To draw out Prickles, see thorns and splinters," "To remedy the pain of the teeth," "To keep garments from moths," and "To cause Hens to lay eggs plentifully." John Gerard's primary interest in plants for the physical benefits they provided for man is understandable, for he was an apothecary, and in 1633 pharmacology, medicine, and botany were inextricably entwined.

Much of Gerard's information about the medicinal virtues of plants was taken from the herbal of Pedacius Dioscorides, a widely traveled soldier from Anazarba in Asia Minor, who lived in the first century A.D. Dioscorides' herbal, the first known book of its kind, was without challenge as a source of plant descriptions and virtues for 1500 years, until the Renaissance stimulated a desire for new and more accurate knowledge. His herbal, however, is considered to be the foundation for our modern sciences of botany and pharmacology.

increased in England and on the Continent in the sixteenth and seventeenth centuries, the botanic gardens of southern Europe acquired cultivated and wild plants and flowers from the countries of the eastern Mediterranean, while the botanic gardens in the port cities of northern Europe drew from the vast store of flower and plant materials from the far-flung colonies that had been recently established in North, South, and Central America, in Africa, and in the Far East. Seeds of Cockscomb and Globe Amaranth accompanied the tea, porcelains, spices, and silks that arrived in Amsterdam from the East Indies, while Tulip, Ranunculus, and Checker Lily bulbs shared a berth in the sailing ships that brought carpets, drugs, and finely worked leathers from Turkey. Among the *Plant It Now, Dry It Later* plants that the American Colonies contributed to European gardens were Maidenhair Fern, Black-eyed Susan, Stokesia, Magnolia, and Mountain Laurel.

Whereas the medicinal virtues of plants familiar to Europeans had been known for hundreds of years, the medicinal virtues of the floral deluge which inundated England and the Continent during these two centuries were impossible to determine. Some plants, such as May Apple, which was used by the American Indians for its vermifugal properties, arrived with notes on their virtues, but the vast majority of plant materials arrived without any descriptive information regarding the plant use (if any) in its native habitat. The exotic beauty of many of these rarities, coupled with the novelty of all of them, resulted in a new appreciation of the beauty of flowers and plants.

The wave of the Renaissance that swept over Europe carried with it the Fashion in Flowers that had existed for so many centuries in the Middle and Far East. "The Turks love to raise all sorts of flowers," the German physician Rauwolf had written in 1574, and in England and on the Continent flower beds and parterres in which plants were grown for the visual beauty of their flowers rapidly replaced the once-popular gardens that had grown plants for their medicinal virtues alone.

Tulip

Angel's Tears Narcissus

One can imagine the pride felt by a wealthy merchant-prince or a head-of-state as he invited friends to view a first flower of its kind to be seen in Europe, produced from a strange seed or bulb from a far-off land. Indeed, competition for the rarest of Tulip bulbs became so keen among the wealthy in Holland that a Tulipomania gripped that nation between 1634 and 1637 which virtually plunged the country into bankruptcy, and it was reported that a collection of exceptionally fine bulbs sold for as much as $44,000!

Many of the rare novelties that were introduced into European flower gardens during the Renaissance became lost in cultivation due to neglect, a lack of understanding of the culture required by the plant, or simply because the plant was unsuited to European climates. Many of these lost beauties were subsequently reintroduced, as was the exquisite Angel's Tears Narcissus *(Narcissus triandrus)*, one of the rare flowers which Jan Brueghel admired and included in his flower paintings in the early seventeenth century. By the end of the seventeenth century this bulb and its flower had disappeared from European gardens and did not reappear until 200 years later when it was discovered growing in its wild state in Spain. It is now a popular and widely cultivated spring flower which I heartily recommend to the gardener interested in drying flowers, and the likelihood of its being lost again in cultivation seems remote.

Flowers were not to be confined for long to the newly established flower beds and parterres. In their proliferation they became a source of design for every decorative art: Parrots, Cockatoos, and other rare birds that arrived in Europe with the rare flowers from faraway places found themselves perched forever on the inlaid floral branches of furniture marquetry and on the painted branches of the Peonies and Roses that seeded themselves on eighteenth-century faience and porcelain. Flowers bloomed in fine tapestries, and in oil and watercolor paintings; they took root in every kind of needlework. Floral garlands and exquisite bouquets bloomed endlessly in the carved and painted salons *en boiserie* in the manoirs and châteaux of France; glass Pansies, Malvas, Crown Imperials, Ipomoeas, Fuchsias, Alliums, and Dahlias bloomed in the paperweights of St. Louis, Baccarat, and Clichy. Through the centuries flowers have proliferated like weeds until today we can scarcely turn without being surrounded by their decorative beauty. All of these efforts, of course, have been attempts to capture the transient beauty of the real flower at its peak of perfection and, as always, Nature plays the coquette, for at no time does a plant have more "come hither" appeal than during the reproductive, or flowering, stage of its life.

Glass Pansy in nineteenth-century paperweight

Today, gardens of flowers in paper, plastic, silk, glass, and jade attempt to provide year-round floral decoration or to supplement the fresh flowers from the local florist garden during the season when the outdoor garden is dormant. Some of these flowers, particularly those made of silk, represent great efforts to recreate in careful detail the beauty of the real flower, while others, such as those made of glass and jade, are, like the ancient carvings, more stylized.

Perhaps the most beautiful of all of these artificial gardens is the Silk Garden of Trousselier, which stands on a corner of the Boulevard Haussmann across from the Louis XVI Square in Paris. It was October when I entered the shop to find red and yellow Tulips, purple and white Lilacs, aqua Scabiosas, and purple and blue Delphiniums blooming from gigantic urns, unmindful that their blooming seasons outdoors had long since ended. Bunches of pink and orange French Primrose, sprays of Roses, blue Hyacinths, and pink and peach-toned Sweet Peas bloomed side by side with yellow and orange Iceland Poppies and bright pink and yellow Gerbera Daisies. Nosegays of tiny flowers, all in silk, were a sharp contrast to the large arrangements. The silk flowers in the Trousselier garden are expensive, and rightly so, for each one is made by hand by adept and artistic women who take great pride in their work.

"What can we do for you?" asked Madame, a tall, viva-

Primrose

cious, energetic woman, who, in response to my reply, bounded through her silk garden searching out the flowers in aqua-tints and rosy-peach tones. I asked where her beautiful blooms were made. "They are made here, of course. Come, let me show you," and I followed Madame's long strides through the café doors to the rear of the shop. Tiers of boxes, carefully labeled to identify their silken contents, lined one wall of the large room, and I found it amusing to reflect on how the catalogings and closetings of flowers, whether they are pressed, processed in silica gel, or made of silk resemble each other.

"When we select a new flower to be made in silk, and this month we are making large Dahlias, it is customary for us to buy from the florist his largest and most beautiful flowers. We give them to three women who dissect each flower to determine its center and the size, shape, and number of petals required to recreate it. We duplicate the petal colors exactly by hand painting on white silk and then we cut the petals to their proper size. Then they are given to those ladies," and Madame waved her hand to encompass some twenty women who sat on either side of four long tables. These artisans work with the most humble of materials: wire, a paste pot, florist's tape, a small white pillow, and furling irons that are kept hot over a gas flame. Only the flat, colorful silk petals offer any hope of beauty. With deft and skillful fingers these bits of silk are transformed into three-dimensional petals which are glued into place along the wire stem. When the flower or bud has been completed its wire stem is pierced into—of all things—a potato, which rides atop a pedestal reminiscent of an aged hatstand. "We have many potatoes at my house!" said Madame. And suddenly the humble potato became a likely possibility as a temporary holder for the wire stems of my own processed flowers as they are removed from the silica gel.

Madame stepped outside with me as I left the shop with my box of aqua-tinted Hyacinths and Scabiosas, and Sweet Peas and Rose buds in shades of rosy-peach. She waved her hand about her in a grand gesture. "During the French Revolution," she said, "the entire area from the Madeline Church to this square was the cemetery for the rich and poor whose heads rolled," and with a quick motion she swept her hand across her throat. "The Square commemorates the cemetery. There, a little history with the flowers! And, with a cheery "Good-bye," and a wave of the hand, she disappeared into her silk garden.

About Names

Plants almost always have two classes of names, their botanical names and their popular names. With the exception of Calendula, Crocus, Dahlia, Freesia, Chrysanthemum, Zinnia, and Anemone (to name but a few plants that have never acquired widely accepted popular names in English and continue to be known only by their botanical names), I have used the popular names in the text because these are the ones with which most gardeners are familiar. However, for the pleasure of the more scientifically oriented gardener, and for those who will enjoy the mental exercise of learning about the family names of plants, the botanical names are listed in the index and alongside the popular name in "Flowers in the Order of Their Appearance in the Garden and Along the Roadside."

> What's in a name? That which we call a Rose
> By any other name would smell as sweet.
>
> [Romeo and Juliet, II-2]

So spoke Juliet from her window to the Capulet orchard, and so every gardener would agree, provided that the "other name" applied to the Rose alone and not to the Onion, too. Now this may sound trivial and hairsplitting, but plants, like people, must have names for universal identification, and our present systematic and standardized method of naming plants has not always existed. Had you been a gardener two hundred and fifty years ago you could never be sure that the plant which you ordered would be the one you would receive.

The present system of naming plants was refined and promoted by the Swedish botanist, Carl von Linné (the Latinized version of his name, Linnaeus, is how he is best known) in the eighteenth century. Prior to his arrival on the botanical scene no single orderly method of naming plants had been universally adopted. One can imagine the confusion in the botanical world of the sixteenth and seventeenth centuries as thousands of new plants arrived in England and on the Continent. How should they be identified? What name should be assigned to each? Who should name them? There were many instances where a single plant had three, four, or more names simply because that number of persons (not necessarily all botanists) had independently named it, and there was no clearinghouse for plant names and identification.

To bring order out of this botanical chaos was the enormous task to which Linnaeus set himself. He tried to sort out all plants on the basis of their sexual characteristics, and his first order of business was to sort the plants by their method of fruition. All those having the same method of fruition were classified as belonging to the same family. From astrology and alchemy he borrowed the ancient symbols ♂ (Mars and iron), ♀ (Venus and copper), ♃ (Jupiter and tin), and assigned to them new meanings to describe certain plant characteristics: ♂ (male), ♀ (female), ♃ (perennial).

Linnaeus did not intend to rename all the plants which already had names, although some were changed, nor did he attempt to eliminate those names that had their roots in the Greek. "Greek family names must inevitably be tolerated," he wrote, "since the science of plants was built up first by the Greeks, or at least it was among the Greeks that it began to lift its head." And so we have poetic allusions, as in *Narcissus*, named for the youth who fell in love with his reflection in a pool of water. The names of consecrated kings and queens continued to be used: Artemisia, wife of King Mansolus, lent her name to a plant with lovely, silvery-green foliage, while Althaea, wife of King Aeneas of Chalcedon, has been botanically memorialized in our beloved Hollyhock.

Ancient physicians continued to be honored by Linnaeus. Achillaea, the disciple of Centaurus, is remembered in the family name for our common and garden Yarrows, while Paeon, physician to Hercules, comes to mind each spring when the gorgeous shrub and herbaceous Peonies are in bloom.

While he tolerated the Greek, it was in Latin, the *lingua franca* of the scientific world, that Linnaeus wrote and lectured to his colleagues throughout Europe. It was natural, then, that the family names which he assigned to the more newly arrived plants have Latin roots. Many were not pure Latin but were Latinized, as was his own name. In selecting these new plant names he considered it a "religious duty" to memorialize the names of botanists "who had advanced the study of botany." Hence, Magnolia, the family name that identifies our beautiful trees with their handsome leaves, honors the French botanist, Pierre Magnol. The Black-eyed Susan and all of her relatives bear the family name of Rudbeckia, in memory of Linnaeus's beloved Professor of Botany at Uppsala College, Olaf Rudbeck.

He refused to name plants in honor of saints or politicians, but tolerated a few European names other than Greek or Latin, namely, the French *Solidago* (Goldenrod) and those which he considered "barbarous," such as *Syringa* (Lilac), and *Lilium* (Lily).

After the family names had been assigned, Linnaeus added specific names which identified the various members within a given family. "A plant has been completely named," said Linnaeus, "when it is furnished with a generic and a specific name."

Sometimes plant names provide personal glimpses of the plant hunters, explorers, and travelers who carried plants and seeds from their native homes to the gardens of Europe. For instance, *Helipterum manglesii*, the botanical names of the pretty everlasting flower, Rhodanthe, reflects a bit of the life of Captain James Mangles of the Royal Navy. A horticulturist and ardent plant enthusiast, Captain Mangles visited his cousin Lady Stirling, wife of the Governor of New Holland (Australia), at Swan River in 1831. He collected some seed during his visit and in subsequent years arranged for several residents of Swan River who were enthusiastic amateur plant hunters to send him consignments of seeds. These he shared with his brother, Robert Mangles, Esq., who grew them in his garden at Sunning Hill.

Some of the seeds sent to Captain Mangles were from plants that were already known in England and on the Continent but others, such as this species of *Helipterum* were new members to their respective known families and, therefore, required specific names. Hence, the plant that was early identified as "Captain Mangles' Rhodanthe" acquired the formal botanical name of *Helipterum manglesii*.

I sometimes marvel at our Western arrogance in naming plants, as if flowers and plants had not existed for anyone before they were discovered by Europeans. But the Chinese had a name for their gorgeous Peony *(moutan)* which they had cultivated for centuries before it was named by the Greeks. And can we be so naive as to think that the new varieties of a native plant developed by Aztec horticulturists for Montezuma's fabled gardens went nameless until Linnaeus conferred upon it "Dahlia" in honor of his pupil, the Swedish botanist, Dr. Andreas Dahl?

Whatever else, today's gardener must be grateful to Linnaeus for bringing order to botanical classification and nomenclature so that now there is little or no confusion about plant names when the gardener orders from the seedsman or nurseryman. The universality of this naming system is important to botanists, too, in that it provides a common scientific language for plant identification around the world. Hence, the botanist in Brazil, England, or Japan

Captain Mangles' Rhodanthe

readily identifies *Chrysanthemum leucanthemum* as our charming Ox-Eye Daisy, regardless of the many local names it may have.

But so much for names. Perhaps as you learn their names your plants will create a personality for your garden which you did not know existed. "If you know not the names, the knowledge of things too is wasted," wrote Isidorius.

About Dry Gardens

In his sixteenth-century garden at Pisa, Luca Ghini developed what has become the art of preserving flowers and plant materials by pressing them between sheets of paper. His specimens were mostly alpine flowers, and these dried, pressed flowers became known as Luca Ghini's *hortus siccus*—dry garden. This method of preserving plant materials became the foundation of the great herbariums, or dried plant-specimen museums, of our modern botanical gardens. The flattened, somewhat two-dimensional specimens are mounted on sheets of paper, catalogued, and closeted, and are rarely seen except by plant scientists.

It became fashionable for the eighteenth-century gentleman of culture to have his own *hortus siccus* in the manner of Luca Ghini. Sometimes these were great volumes representing extensive plant collecting wherein a wealthy man might even retain a botanical artist to portray his collected plant materials, but more often they were small, personal volumes in which plants and flowers, carefully pressed by the owner, were meticulously mounted. Of great importance was the proper identification of each plant specimen according to the recently introduced Linnean system of botanical nomenclature. Usually noted, too, were the geographical sources of the mounted plants and flowers, their flowering times and relative abundance, and other bits of information the collector deemed important.

Thanks to new methods of preserving flowers, we are more fortunate than Luca Ghini and the dry garden enthusiasts who followed him. Our *horti sicci*—our dry gardens—need not be flattened and tucked away between sheets of paper; their three-dimensional beauty can be ever on display for all to enjoy!

Flowers are fleeting, and before Luca Ghini developed his method of pressing plant specimens to preserve them the only way that the beauty and characteristics of flowers and plant materials could be retained was by drawing them in accurate detail. Although pressing permitted plant materials to be preserved for study it often did not satisfactorily convey the true beauty of the three-dimensional living plant or flower, which continued to be better portrayed by a botanical artist. One senses, then, the total frustration Linnaeus must have felt at the end of one growing season in his botanical garden in Uppsala when he despaired, "There is in the whole of Uppsala not a soul who can make a careful figure. I had in summer over 150 new admirable flowers which must pass into oblivion." What Linnaeus might not have given for our modern methods of preserving flowers!

As you dry a part of your summer garden you will begin to develop a new dimension to your thinking as you realize, as I did, that your *hortus siccus*—your dry garden—has no season! And your carefully stored boxes of dried flowers suddenly bring to life the philosophical garden of the Middle Ages—the Garden of Paradise, or Mary's Garden, where all flowers supposedly bloomed together. Your dried-flower arranging, then, takes on an almost infinite number of possibilities as you draw from a garden whose variety is unlimited by season and is as broad as the variety of flowers and plant materials you choose to dry.

Famous Flower Paintings and Floral Fashions of Other Eras

While John Gerard saw plants first as the "meate of men, then for medicine to recover health," there were other men of his time who saw plants for the beauty of their flowers alone. Across the North Sea the Flemish artists, and particularly Jan Brueghel the Elder, had begun to apply paint to wood to create the first paintings of floral arrangements as we know them today. He traveled far and wide to the private gardens of the wealthy merchant-princes to study and sketch the rare plants and flowers newly arrived in Europe, and he was often invited to paint the rare beauties growing in the gardens of Archduke Albert and Isabella in Brussels. Jan was meticulous in his detail and his paintings are masterpieces of botanical accuracy.

Some of Brueghel's arrangements, such as *Flowers in a Blue Vase,* are compositions of spring flowers only, while others are of flowers which bloom at various times during the growing season. There has been some speculation about whether the latter are composites of drawings, or whether Jan was trying to recreate the medieval philosophical Garden of Paradise, or Mary's Garden. Rather than being philosophical, however, I suspect that Brueghel took great pride in his work and was eager to show the many rare beauties he had painted without regard to their blooming period, for he wrote to his friend, Cardinal Borromeo, Archbishop of Milan, in 1606: "Flowers, all of them painted after nature: in this picture I have painted everything that I am

Jan Brueghel's *Flowers in a Blue Vase* (Figure 2)

able to do. I believe that never before have so many rare and diverse flowers been painted and with such painstaking care." Whatever his philosophy, Jan Brueghel earned his living from the sale of his paintings, and of those of floral arrangements he wrote: "In winter they will provide a nice view."

The sketches and paintings of Jan Brueghel and other artists of his time, fashioned after living plants and un-picked flowers in the gardens where they grew, were meticulously put together with paint on wood in those informal arrangements that are models of Flemish floral artistry.

Except for botanical artists, flower painters in subsequent centuries were not always so painstaking in their detail as Jan Brueghel and his contemporaries. Also, their paintings were often of arrangements of freshly picked flowers. There were pitfalls here, too, for the conscientious artist, and Vincent Van Gogh once wrote: "I am working every morning from sunrise, for flowers fade so soon and the thing is to do the whole at a flash."

Regardless of their method or the detail of their floral painting, the Brueghels, Van Goghs, and other flower artists all reflect the fashions in flowers and floral arrangements of their day, and their wall hangings are permanent records of real, but transient, flowers. How exciting, then, to consider that the process can now be reversed, and that flower paintings and the floral fashions of other eras can be recreated (albeit somewhat modified at times) with dried flowers that, to paraphrase Brueghel, in winter they will provide a nice view.

"But," you may ask, "are the rare and exotic flowers which Brueghel chose to paint more than 350 years ago available to us today?" The answer, of course, is "Yes!" For instance, the rare flowers, such as Tulip, Daffodil, Checker Lily, and Anemone, which appealed most to his artist's eye in 1600 and which he selected to show among some of the common flowers of the time, are the very flowers that appeal most to the home gardener today. We are more fortunate than Jan Brueghel, however, in that we need not travel great distances to private and botanical gardens to enjoy their beauty. Virtually all of Brueghel's rare flowers are beauties as readily available to the American gardener from American seedsmen and nurserymen as they are to the Parisian who buys his seeds and bulbs from the seed shops on the Quai de Gesvres along the Seine, or to the English gardener who supplements his garden beauty from the open stalls on Market Day in Cambridge.

One autumn day, I called on a local Holland bulb importer with a copy of Brueghel's painting under my arm to purchase the Snowflake, Narcissus, Checker Lily and Tulip bulbs whose flowers I planned to dry the following spring to recreate *Flowers in a Blue Vase*. I showed the importer the painting and asked him which varieties of Tulip he would suggest to approximate most closely the colors and forms of the flowers in the painting.

"I think this is Comet, one of our new ones," he said, pointing to the yellow parrot Tulip edged in red. "This is Mariette," and he indicated the pink Lily-flowered Tulip, "and this white Lily-flowered Tulip is Triumphator." His pleasure at being able to offer the "new varieties" shown in the painting left me with little heart to tell him that the brightly colored flower arrangement we were looking at had been painted more than 350 years ago! But the experience proved, once again, how truly international is the beauty of our American garden.

In 1730, nurseryman Robert Furber issued in London his *Twelve Months of Flowers,* a folio containing twelve prints of floral arrangements, one for each month of the year. These prints are favorites of visitors to the restored area of Williamsburg, Virginia, and modern reproductions have made them among the most popular floral prints in use in American homes today. Furber's pictures were not intended as wall hangings of actual flower arrangements; rather, they were issued as an elegant seed and plant catalogue of the flowers cultivated in London gardens in the

"June" from Robert Furber's *Twelve Months of Flowers* (Figure 3)

eighteenth century which the "gardiner of Kensington" had for sale in his nursery. His catalog was intended as

> ... a means of informing the Publick of the great Variety of Flowers, in all their Stations, at every season of the Year. It may be thought, perhaps, that the Winter Months are void of the Delights expected in a Flower-Garden; but the Mistake will soon be discover'd by a curious Observer, when he shall find, that there are at least Two and Thirty Flowers of different Kinds then in their Splendour.

The Flemish artist, Peter Casteels, was commissioned to illustrate this novel catalogue. Like Brueghel one hundred years before, Casteels probably painted the flowers, "coloured to the life," from sketches or as they grew in gardens, arranging them in urns and vases only with his paints, for on close inspection we find flowers such as Primroses and Mallows that were no more appropriate for fresh flower arranging in the eighteenth century than they are today. Dried flowers, however, offer the rare opportunity to recreate an eighteenth-century arrangement of flowers that never really existed—except in the eye of the artist.

If your decorating taste is eighteenth-century English or Colonial Williamsburg, consult Furber's *Twelve Months of Flowers* and plan your garden to include some of the flowers that bloomed in London gardens at that time. Furber's flowers were arranged to show the flowers in bloom during each month of the year. Your dry garden, however, *has no season,* and your arranging is not confined to any one of Furber's monthly selections. You may choose freely from any and all of his *Twelve Months* to create your own arrangement, perhaps in the manner of Casteels, of true eighteenth-century floral fashion.

Among the many flowers that can be dried that appear in Furber's catalogue are Christmas Rose, Goldenrod, Larkspur, Checker Lily, Cockscomb, and many varieties of

Daffodil, Anemone, and Tulip. Furber indexed the names of his flowers below each arrangement for the convenience of his customers, but some of his names vary slightly from the names in use today, because Furber's catalog was issued before Linnaeus introduced his standardized method of naming plants in 1753. For instance, Furber's White Eternal is our Pearly Everlasting *(Anaphalis margaritacea);* his Purple Amaranthoides is our magenta Globe Amaranth *(Gomphrena globosa);* and his Perennial Dwarf Sunflower, our Black-eyed Susan *(Rudbeckia hirta).* See "Recreation of Famous Flower Paintings and Floral Fashions of Other Eras" for currently popular names of other Furber offerings.

Claude Monet's *Sunflowers* (Figure 4)

Sunflowers were popular "cottage flowers" in England and Europe after their arrival from Mexico in the sixteenth century and, undoubtedly, were often cut for use as indoor floral decoration. Plant them and gather them from your own garden or from the roadside to recreate Claude Monet's *Sunflowers,* at right, to complement the provincial furnishings of every era.

Some Plant It Now, Dry It Later Flower Surprises

Drying a part of your garden can give you a variety of flowers for arrangements unmatched by any florist. For instance, dwarf varieties of Aster which I often use to edge the annual border have very limited use indoors as cut flowers because of their short stems, but their use is widely extended after they have been wired and dried.

Some outdoor beauties never make their way indoors in a freshly cut state for another reason: Mallows, Hollyhocks, and Rose of Sharon are almost useless in a fresh bouquet because, in addition to their exceedingly short stems, the cut flowers bloom on the stalk or branch for only a very short time. Wired and dried, however, these flowers add bright new interest to your indoor floral decoration.

The Crocus is an unlikely subject for fresh flower arranging, and all but the most ingenious arranger might throw up his hands if requested to do anything more with a Primrose than pot it for indoor use. But you have only to look at Fig. 15 to appreciate the beauty the Crocus offers when dried; and Primrose, dried, becomes an important ingredient in the recreation of Furber's eighteenth-century floral compositions.

Clematis is a great and showy vine outdoors, but who has attempted to place this beautiful flower in a fresh bouquet?

Dog's Tooth Violet, Lenten Rose, and the May Apple, with its head hidden beneath its leaves, provide but a moment of wild flower pleasure in the span of a growing

season. When dried, they can be enjoyed and studied for
many months. These are among the many surprises that
can reward your planting and drying efforts.

The range of flowers available for drying is as universal
as any seedsman's or nurseryman's catalogue. As in the
catalogues, there may be a few variations in gardening
suggestions or plant classifications because of variations in
climate. Some of the plant materials which I recommend for
your gardening pleasure, such as Acacia and Eucalyptus,
do not grow in my garden in northern New Jersey because
they do not survive the cold of winter. If your climate is
warmer than mine, some of these plants, for which I am
dependent upon my local florist, may grow in your own
backyard. Other plants which I grow as annuals, such as
Verbena and Cockscomb, are grown as perennials in the
south.

The division between those plants that I consider
"cultivated" and those I consider "wild" (including weeds)
may be disputed elsewhere in the world, but one must
always keep in mind that all plants have been native to one
part of the globe or another, and plants that are too common
for one man's garden are often treasured in the garden of
another. An English friend who lives in the suburbs of
London is forever weeding her lawn to free it from that
"annoying Anemone" while three thousand miles away I
coax my spring-planted corms into flower with the tenderest
of care! Conversely, although I enjoy the beauty of Goldenrod, it is such a common roadside plant in northern New
Jersey that it will never be more than a weed to my mind,
even though in recent years it has been given prominent
billing in some of our foremost nurserymen's catalogues
under its botanical name, *Solidago.*

Greater scientific accuracy would have been served if
what I have termed the "family" name of plants had been
referred to as genera. However, I have elected to take the
less scientifically accurate route in an effort to personalize
the garden and personify its flowers. The popular names

of the plants are in roman type; their family and specific names, as well as the variety, where included, are italicized.

Where I have dried only one member of a family I have noted its specific name except in those cases such as *Trollius* where the species was uncertain. Here, *sp.,* the botanist's abbreviation for *species,* in the singular, is used to denote this uncertainty. This is not to say that other members of these many families cannot be dried successfully, but rather that a lack of time and/or their availability made further experimentation impossible. For example, the Sunflower *(Helianthus)* family has many members that grow in great profusion over most of the United States. Only the annual Sunflower *(Helianthus annuus)* has been included in this book, although I suspect many others should dry beautifully.

Where two or more members of the same family have been dried successfully, I have used *spp.* to denote *species,* in the plural. Wherever possible, the species and variety are further identified in "Flowers in the Order of Their Appearance in the Garden and Along the Roadside."

But these are small matters. *Plant It Now, Dry It Later* has been written for your reading, gardening, and decorative pleasure. It is hoped that your spirit will feel the same surge of joy from preserving the colorful treasures of your garden that I have experienced from preserving mine.

In addition to the plants whose flowers, fruits, and foliage are included here, there are many other colorful flowers that are waiting eagerly to be processed so that they, too, may flaunt their beauty in your dried bouquet. So cast your gardening and drying timidity aside; grow some plants that may be new to you, and dry some of your own favorites that may not be included here. As you experiment with new flowers to add to your dry garden, record your findings on the page designed for this purpose that follows "Flowers in the Order of Their Appearance in the Garden and along the Roadside." Your success will be a source of unbounded joy.

Plant It Now

Things You'll Need To Plant It Now: Things You'll Need To Dry It Later

Planting now and drying later require a minimal investment in materials and equipment. The small investment is more than offset by the beauty and pleasure derived from your dried flowers.

PLANTING NOW:

If you already have a garden there is probably available the
    fork,
    hoe,
    hose,
    and pruners.
You may even save the bamboo plant stakes to use from year to year as I do.
    Seeds and
    plants,
    fertilizer, and
    lime
are anticipated annual investments. The key to successful flower drying, of course, lies in the selection of the seeds and plants that will produce the flowers best for drying. Browse through the sections on the Lazy Flowers, the More Effort Flowers, or the "Flowers in the Order of Their Appearance in the Garden and Along the Roadside" to choose those whose form and color appeal most to you.

DRYING LATER: 5 pounds of silica gel to dry the More Effort Flowers. The quantity really depends on how much processing you plan to do and which flowers you wish to dry. Obviously, a large spray of Delphinium requires more silica gel for processing than a Rose or two. But it is best to start small and achieve success with a few flowers rather than failure with many. As you refine your technique for drying the More Effort Flowers your enthusiasm will increase, and you, too, may be drying almost everything in sight. At that point, invest in another

    5 pounds of silica gel

Drying the More Effort Flowers also requires

    1 spool #23 wire
    1 spool #26 wire

The last is not always available from the florist but can usually be found in electronic supply shops. Rather than the dull florist-green enamel finish it is often a bright green but this is of little importance, for it is either wrapped with tape or is so situated in the arrangement that it cannot be seen.

    1 small, otherwise unused, sauce pan to hold
    ½ block paraffin, which, when melted, is applied with
      a
    cotton Q-tip to the underside of a few flowers to
      strengthen them where the petals meet the stem
    a few cake tins or other tins with tight-fitting lids
    coat hangers
    snips for cutting wire and stems

(I use my small Wilkinson Sword pruners to prune both the living stems of the plants in my garden and the wire stems of my dried flowers. This might appall those who take pride in things such as pruners but the pruners appear to have suffered no ill effects from the double life they have led.)

    glycerin, for processing foliages

oasis and/or styrofoam
sand
1 roll brown florist's tape
1 roll green florist's tape
Posey Klay
lengths of #10 and #18 wire
kenzan, or needlepoint holder, if the arrangement
 requires one
the same pruners

If you wish to dry large quantities of flowers in silica gel and you live in an area where the summer humidity often soars above seventy percent it would be wise to consider investing in a dehumidifier to assure their successful summer storage. If your anticipated drying is limited to smaller quantities, select most of your materials from the Lazy Flowers and a few from the More Effort Flowers that bloom later in the growing season. This kind of careful selection will provide you with an abundance of dried materials for your own, and your friends', pleasure. Also, read carefully the section on how to store the More Effort Flowers.

OTHER THINGS YOU WILL NEED FOR ARRANGING:

The Plant It Now, Dry It Later Gardens

Although John Gerard considered visual beauty as secondary to the more useful attributes of a plant, he was not oblivious to the beauty of the plants and flowers in his own garden, and he offers what can only be interpreted as encouragement to those of us who garden for visual pleasure: "For if delight may provoke mens labor, what greater delight is there than to behold the earth apparelled with plants, and garnished with great diversities of rare and costly jewels?"

Gerard's early seventeenth-century London garden did not sparkle with nearly so many of the earth's jewels as our American garden does today. Many of our most beautiful garden plants, such as Azalea and Hydrangea, were unknown to him, and some of his favorites, such as Snapdragon and Purple-Floure Gentle, might be reluctant to acknowledge their progeny, for cultivation and hybridization during the past few centuries have developed flowers that are sometimes larger, or that have a different color, or even a slightly different form from their ancestors. For example, the Snapdragon, a plant particularly responsive to horticultural efforts, was forced to a grotesque height of six feet in late Victorian England. More recently, variations in its form have been developed, identified by such names as Butterfly and Bellflower.

Gerard's "Purple-Floure Gentle"

Gerard's Purple-Floure Gentle is the plumed Celosia of today, and I cannot help but wonder what accommodation he might make to its name if he were to view its golden plumes in my garden.

You may find, as I have, that capturing the transient beauty of the garden at the peak of its blooming perfection adds a new dimension to your gardening. How often I have waited with eager anticipation for the Tulips to come into flower only to have an unseasonable heat wave curl their petals, and with a sigh I have resigned myself to waiting another 360 days to enjoy their beauty again! Now, however, I dry a few pink and white "Her Grace" Tulips as they come into bloom and store them until the garden is dormant. As the growing season advances I dry other favorites as they appear: the purple Anemone and rose and pink Peonies in May and June, pink Roses, pink and white Summer Phlox, and Delphinium during the summer. With a few Beech leaves processed in July and August, and some sprays of Eucalyptus from the florist, this garden beauty blooms untiringly throughout the winter months. (Fig. 11.)

When selecting your garden plants, choose those whose flowers, fruits, seeds, and foliage will provide you with the forms and colors you most like to live with. My summer garden always includes a wide variety of the Lazy Flowers in shades of pink, purple, yellow, and white. These flowers retain their fresh appearance regardless of a high reading on the humidistat, and so I prefer to use them in bath and powder rooms, and in other places for year-round decoration.

It is not necessary to garden on a grand scale to enjoy the delights of dried arrangements. A few well-chosen plants will produce enough flowers (or fruits or seeds or foliage) for several arrangements. For instance, one plant each of yellow and orange Marigolds and magenta Globe Amaranth will yield more than enough flowers for several arrangements like the one in Fig. 9. Single plants of Japanese

Bamboo, Shasta Daisy, and Chrysanthemum that fruit and flower in the fall will provide enough fruits and flowers to create arrangements like the one in Fig. 10 for yourself and several friends. A single healthy plant of Black-Eyed Susans will produce more than enough flowers to recreate a modified version of Claude Monet's *Sunflowers*.

All of the Lazy and More Effort Flowers suggested for you to grow in your own garden to dry later are listed below. Some of them may be old favorites and it may come as something of a surprise that their flowers or other parts can be brought indoors for colorful winter decoration. Develop a gardening spirit of adventure: Grow some of the plants with which you are not familiar, and let them open doors of new beauty for you.

ANNUALS

ACROCLINIUM *(Helipterum roseum)*
CELOSIA, PLUMED *(Celosia argentea)*
CHENILLE PLANT *(Acalypha hispida)*
COCKSCOMB *(Celosia cristata)*
CORN, ORNAMENTAL *(Zea mays* var. *japonica)*
GLOBE AMARANTH *(Gomphrena globosa)*
ORNAMENTAL GRASSES *(various families)*

RHODANTHE *(Helipterum manglesii)*
SALVIA, SUMMER *(Salvia farinacea)*
STATICE *(Limonium sinuatum)*
STRAWFLOWER *(Helichrysum bracteatum)*
WHEAT *(Triticum aestivum)*
WINGED EVERLASTING *(Ammobium alatum)*
XERANTHEMUM *(Xeranthemum annuum)*

THE LAZY FLOWERS

BIENNIALS

HONESTY *(Lunaria annua)*

PERENNIALS

BABY'S-BREATH *(Gypsophila paniculata)*

CATTAIL *(Typha* spp)

CHINESE LANTERN (Physalis
  alkekengi)
CHIVE (Allium schoenoprasum)
EULALIA (Miscanthus sinensis
  var. gracillima)
GLOBE THISTLE (Echinops sp)
GOLDENROD (Solidago spp)
JAPANESE BAMBOO (Polygonum
  sieboldii)
LAVENDER (Lavandula sp)

PEARLY EVERLASTING (Ana-
  phalis margaritacea)
PLUME GRASS (Erianthus raven-
  nae)
SEA HOLLY (Eryngium amethy-
  stinum)
SEA LAVENDER (Limonium
  latifolium)
TANSY (Tanacetum vulgare)
YARROW (Achillea spp)

SHRUBS
HEATH (Erica spp)
HEATHER (Calluna vulgaris)
PUSSY WILLOW (Salix discolor)

TREES
ACACIA (Acacia spp)
BIRCH, BLACK (Betula carpini-
  folia)

VINES
BITTERSWEET (Celastrus spp)

THE MORE EFFORT FLOWERS

ANNUALS
ASTER, CHINA (Callistephus
  chinensis)
BABY'S-BREATH (Gypsophila
  elegans)
BACHELOR'S BUTTON (Centa-
  urea cyanus)
BELLS OF IRELAND (Moluccella
  laevis)
CALENDULA (Calendula offi-
  cinalis)
CANDYTUFT (Iberis spp)
CARNATION (Dianthus spp)
DAHLIA (Dahlia spp)
GERANIUM (Pelargonium zonale)
LARKSPUR (Delphinium ajacis)

MARIGOLD (Tagetes spp)
PANSY (Viola spp)
PINCUSHION FLOWER (Scabiosa
  atropurpurea)
POPPY, CORN (Papaver rhoeas)
POPPY, OPIUM (Papaver somni-
  ferum)
SNAPDRAGON (Antirrhinum
  majus)
STOCK (Matthiola incana var.
  annua)
SUNFLOWER (Helianthus
  annuus)
VERBENA (Verbena spp)
ZINNIA (Zinnia elegans)

BIENNIALS

CANTERBURY BELLS *(Campanula medium)*
HOLLYHOCK *(Althaea rosea)*
PANSY *(Viola* spp)
STOCK *(Matthiola incana)*
THISTLE *(Cirsium* spp)

PERENNIALS

ALKANET *(Anchusa officinalis)*
ASTER, NEW ENGLAND *(Aster novae-angliae)*
BELLFLOWER *(Platycodon grandiflorum)*
BLACK-EYED SUSAN *(Rudbeckia hirta)*
BLUE/WHITE BONNET *(Scabiosa caucasica)*
CANDYTUFT *(Iberis sempervirens)*
CARNATION and PINK *(Dianthus* spp)
CHRISTMAS ROSE *(Helleborus niger)*
CHRYSANTHEMUM *(Chrysanthemum* spp)
COLUMBINE *(Aquilegia vulgaris)*
DANDELION *(Taraxacum officinale)*
DAY LILY *(Hemerocallis* spp)
DELPHINIUM *(Delphinium* spp)
DOG'S-TOOTH VIOLET *(Erythronium americanum)*
FEVERFEW *(Chrysanthemum parthenium)*
GLOBE THISTLE *(Echinops* sp)
GLOBEFLOWER *(Trollius* sp)
GOLDENROD *(Solidago* spp)
HARDY AGERATUM *(Eupatorium coelestinum)*
HARDY CYCLAMEN *(Cyclamen neapolitanum)*
IRIS *(Iris* spp)
IRONWEED *(Vernonia noveborecensis)*
LENTEN ROSE *(Helleborus orientalis)*
MAY APPLE *(Podophyllum peltatum)*
OX-EYE DAISY *(Chrysanthemum leucanthemum)*
PAINTED DAISY *(Chrysanthemum coccineum)*
PEONY *(Paeonia* spp)
POPPY, ICELAND *(Papaver nudicaule)*
POPPY, ORIENTAL *(Papaver orientale)*
PHLOX *(Phlox divaricata* and *Phlox paniculata)*
PRIMROSE *(Primula* spp)
ROCK CRESS *(Arabis alpina)*
SEA HOLLY *(Eryngium amethystinum)*
SHASTA DAISY *(Chrysanthemum maximum)*
STOKE'S ASTER *(Stokesia laevis)*
SWEET ROCKET *(Hesperis matronalis)*
WILD GERANIUM *(Geranium* spp)

SHRUBS

AZALEA *(Rhododendron* spp)
BRIDAL WREATH *(Spiraea* spp)
DOGWOOD *(Cornus florida)*
GUELDER ROSE *(Viburnum opulus* var. *sterilis)*
HYDRANGEA *(Hydrangea macrophylla)*
LILAC *(Syringa* spp)
PEONY *(Paeonia moutan)*
RHODODENDRON *(Rhododendron* spp)
ROSE *(Rosa* spp)
ROSE OF SHARON *(Hibiscus syriacus)*

TREES

DOGWOOD *(Cornus florida)*
HAWTHORN *(Crataegus oxyacantha* var, *paulii)*
REDBUD *(Cercis canadensis)*

VINES

CLEMATIS *(Clematis* spp)
PASSIONFLOWER *(Passiflora caerulea)*

BULBS AND CORMS

ANEMONE *(Anemone coronaria)*
CHECKER LILY *(Fritillaria meleagris)*
CHIVE, CHINESE *(Allium tuberosum)*
CROCUS *(Crocus* spp)
CROWN IMPERIAL *(Fritillaria imperialis)*
DAFFODIL *(Narcissus* spp)
FREESIA *(Freesia refracta)*
GLADIOLUS *(Gladiolus* spp)
GLORY-OF-THE-SNOW *(Chionodoxa luciliae* and others)
LILY *(Lilium* spp)
RANUNCULUS *(Ranunculus asiaticus)*
SNOWFLAKE *(Leucojum* spp)
SQUILL *(Scilla sibirica* and others)
TULIP *(Tulipa* spp)

FOLIAGE

ANNUAL

SNOW-ON-THE-MOUNTAIN *(Euphorbia marginata)*

PERENNIALS

DUSTY MILLER/ARTEMISIA
(*Artemisia stelleriana*)
GROUND PINE (*Lycopodium
obscurum*)

HARDY CYCLAMEN (*Cyclamen
neapolitanum*)
MAIDENHAIR FERN (*Adiantum
spp*)

SHRUBS

AZALEA (*Rhododendron* spp)
BOXWOOD (*Buxus japonica*)
IVY (*Hedera helix*)
JUNIPER (*Juniperus communis
var. depressa*)
LILAC (*Syringa* spp)
MOUNTAIN LAUREL (*Kalmia
latifolia*)

OREGON HOLLY GRAPE (*Maho-
nia aquifolium*)
PEONY (*Paeonia* spp)
RHODODENDRON (*Rhododen-
dron* spp)
ROSE (*Rosa* spp)
SCOTCH BROOM (*Cytisus
scoparius*)

TREES

BEECH (*Fagus* spp)
DEVILWOOD (*Osmanthus
americanus*)
DOGWOOD (*Cornus florida*)
EUCALYPTUS/SILVER DOLLAR
TREE (*Eucalyptus cinerea*)
FLOWERING CRABAPPLE
(*Malus* sp)
HOLLY (*Ilex opaca*)

LILY-OF-THE-VALLEY-TREE
(*Oxydendrum arboreum*)
MAGNOLIA (*Magnolia grandi-
flora*)
PEAR (*Pyrus communis*)
PIN OAK (*Quercus palustris*)
PURPLE PLUM (*Prunus cerasi-
fera* var. *pissardii*)

VINES

PASSIONFLOWER (*Passiflora
caerulea*)

Annuals are the plants whose entire life cycle, seed to flower to seed, is completed in a single growing season. They are a "must" in the sunny border where they provide masses of color throughout the summer. They are important, too, for the new home where the young, permanent planting often

*HOW DOES YOUR
GARDEN GROW?*

looks rather sparse. Among the *Plant It Now, Dry It Later* annuals are Aster, Cockscomb, Globe Amaranth, Sunflower, Marigold, Zinnia, and Verbena.

Biennials are those plants whose life cycle spans two years. The seed is planted the first year and the plants flower and seed in the second year. *Plant It Now, Dry It Later* biennials include Honesty and Canterbury Bells.

Perennials are the backbone of one's garden for these are the plants which, once established, yield their beauty with average care year after year. Many of the *Plant It Now, Dry It Later* perennials such as Baby's-Breath, Black-Eyed Susan, Peony, Globe Thistle, and Lavender may already be in your garden, and it may come as something of a surprise that they can be carried indoors for your wintertime enjoyment.

Shrubs are the woody plants which are smaller than trees and, unlike trees, have two or more trunks. The shrubs useful to the *Plant It Now, Dry It Later* gardener for their foliage, flowers, or fruit include Azalea, Rose of Sharon, Devilwood, and Pussy Willow.

Trees included here are ornamental and are useful for their blossoms, foliage, or fruit. Hawthorn and Dogwood are delightful in the border or as lawn specimens, while others, such as the Purple and Copper Beeches, are great shade trees which perform their services as lawn specimens and patio coolers.

Among the *Bulbs* suggested for your planting and drying pleasure are Crocus, Tulip, Daffodil, and Checker Lily. Bittersweet and Clematis are among the climbing plants or *Vines* that are marvelous on walls and fences, and in the dried bouquet.

Consider your soil and climate before ordering your seeds and plants, and then grow the plants most suited to the planting area. While it is always rewarding to achieve success with a plant alien to its situation it is not wise to plan an entire garden around these specialties. Too often the results do not justify the effort and time involved, and the summer garden is a disappointment. It is far better to concentrate on those flowers which will grow well in your soil and which will reward you with an abundant harvest and particularly happy wintertime memories.

Consider, too, your motivation as a gardener as well as a flower dryer and arranger when selecting your plants. The garden cared for by the best intentions will provide the poorest harvest if the gardener is absent during most of the growing season. If you spend your summer away from home plan you garden around those flowers and plant materials that can be harvested and stored during the spring and fall when you are there to care for them.

ANNUALS, BIENNIALS, AND PERENNIALS.

Local nurserymen usually sell a variety of annuals (and some biennials and perennials) in flats or boxes or pots. Buying the plants rather than growing them from seed has some advantages, particularly in the case of annuals whose flowering season may be extended, thereby assuring you of a maximum number of blooms from the plant. Unfortunately, your chances of finding all of the Lazy and More Effort plants at a local nursery are very slim. Flower growers tend to grow the old favorites, the Zinnias, Marigolds, Dahlias, and others with which American gardeners are most familiar. These are wonderful, showy plants for beds and borders. They are easy to grow and are prolific in their flowering. However, there are many other flowers than can add great beauty and variety to your garden, and these should not be overlooked. It is hard to say whether gardeners or growers are more responsible for the lack of variety available locally to most American home gardeners. It is a little like the chicken and the egg. The gardener does not buy what he is not familiar with, and the grower, reluctant to gamble with his income, grows only those plants he knows he can sell. Perhaps *Plant It Now, Dry It Later* will give both gardener and nurseryman a new and broader awareness of the garden beauty available to us if we but make a small effort to seek it out.

WHERE WILL YOUR PLANTS COME FROM?

If your growing season is short, or the prospects of getting an early start on your seeds seems dim, approach a local nurseryman about starting the seeds of your choice in his greenhouse. Garden groups might place quantity orders in advance. A nurseryman, like any other good businessman, is gratified to have orders that will insure his income. In any event, ask him in December to try a flat or two of Globe Amaranth, Statice, and Bells of Ireland. You may open doors of interest for him, too.

If you cannot arrange to buy your plants or to have the seed started locally, consult the catalogues of the reliable seedsmen who carry out their business through the mails. Their catalogues are generally excellent sources of gardening information, and they make wonderful reading on a long winter night.

TREES AND SHRUBS, BULBS AND VINES.
Many of these are available from your local nurseryman, but, like the annuals and perennials, the choice is often limited to those plants and bulbs that are best known. Consult nurserymen's catalogues for plants which you may not be able to order locally.

*GIVING YOUR SEED
A "HEAD START"*

Growing your own plants from seed can be a tremendously rewarding experience. The seed may be started in a variety of ways. Most seedsmen offer equipment (lights, trays, potting mediums, and pots) to give the gardener the opportunity to start his seed indoors during the winter. If you are an African Violet addict and grow your plants under lights, shift the pots slightly to make room to start your seed.

Outdoor cold frames are also wonderful for starting seed, and heated greenhouses offer unlimited possibilities to the gardener. Not many gardeners have the resources of a greenhouse, however, and few are so resourceful as my friend the Major, who constructed his greenhouse of the glass

photographic plates from yesterday's newspapers and maga-
zines. He starts his seed in January and the winter sun
streams through Goya's *Don Manuel*, Bulova watches,
scantily clad Scandale's models, and the Jolly Green Giant
and his Niblets to nurture some 10,000 plants that provide
the riot of color that is his summer garden.

*GROWING SEED
WITHOUT A
"HEAD START"*

If you are a "plain-dirt" gardener as I am and have no equipment available to give your seed a head start, begin your
seed outdoors in a bed prepared as recommended in "Dig
Your Garden" when the ground is warm and the danger of
frost is passed. I often start my own annuals and some
perennials in this manner with considerable success.

*DIG YOUR GARDEN:
GENERAL
GARDENING HINTS*

In selecting a site for your flower bed bear in mind that
many flowers turn their heads to the sun, and so a border
which faces south will be most satisfactory; those facing east
and west will also do well, but you may feel slighted if your
border faces north, for your flowers may have their heads
turned away from you all summer!

Most of the plants in the *Plant It Now, Dry It Later* gardens require a sunny situation and a well-drained soil that
will permit roots to grow freely.

ANNUAL BEDS require soil preparation in the spring
for the most vigorous plant growth. Prepare your annual,
or new perennial, bed as follows:

1. Cover the area with an inch or two of humus (peat
   moss, rotted manure, or decayed leaves and grass
   clippings). This will help a too-sandy soil to retain
   moisture longer and will help to break up a claylike
   soil to permit maximum root development.
2. Add a good general fertilizer, 5-10-5 or 6-10-4, to
   the humus at the rate of 1 to 1¼ pounds for every
   100 square feet of garden area.
3. Till the soil, the humus, and the fertilizer to a depth

of a garden fork, or about eight inches. Tilling should be done when the soil is dry; if tilled when wet the soil becomes more compact, thereby providing less aeration and retarding root development.

4. If necessary, rake in ground limestone to sweeten the soil. The amount of limestone used depends on the soil requirements. If you are uncertain as to its needs, it is a simple matter to have the soil tested or to test it yourself. Soil testing is a service which is provided by your county or state agricultural agent. If you prefer to do it yourself the Green Thumb Soil Test Kit, packaged by the Sudbury Laboratories, Sudbury, Massachusetts, makes it easy to determine the chemical needs of your soil.

5. Level the soil with a rake before planting the seeds or plants.

Established perennial beds need nourishment in the spring, too, so sprinkle some of your garden fertilizer around these plants. Divide the perennials which are increased by the division of their roots when the clumps become large. Shasta Daisies, Globe Thistle, and Chrysanthemums should be divided every few years if they are to retain their beauty and size. There are other perennials such as the Lenten Rose and the Christmas Rose that prefer to have their roots left undisturbed, so check the preference of the plant before you dig.

All flower beds, whether they are for annual or perennial plants, require a good water supply near at hand. Use the water wisely. *Do not* sprinkle; *do* soak to a depth of six inches. Remember that roots develop to meet the water supplied to them so water deeply to encourage deep rooting. Surface watering encourages surface rooting and plants so rooted are susceptible to damage during hot, dry summer periods.

Finally, let the nourishment of your garden soil feed your flowers, not the weeds. Pull them out as they appear.

GROUPING THE PLANTS of each variety together for masses of color is far more effective than the one here, one there, kind of planting. Even if you have only a half dozen Zinnia plants, set them together so that their color and/or common form reinforce each other.

In my own garden I like the continuity of border planting and often my flower beds are edged in Burpee's Nugget Marigolds or Park's dwarf crested Celosia which bloom on and on through the growing season and then come indoors with me to avoid the chills of winter. Dwarf varieties of many taller favorites such as Asters and Zinnias have been developed which offer the gardener an ever-widening variety of border plants to choose from.

THINNING and TRANSPLANTING. Thin your seedlings out before they get too "leggy." Clusters of seedlings tend to use their energy in growing tall instead of growing strong so it is important to thin them out when they are about two inches tall (or as directed by the seedsman) to produce the sturdiest plants.

Transplanting is a traumatic experience for plants, and you will be assured of the greatest success if your seedlings are separated and transplanted on a damp, cloudy day. Resist the temptation of setting the seedlings too close together for an instant mass effect. Give them sufficient space and the plants will be stronger, and their flowers larger and better formed.

Some plants, such as Chrysanthemums, Snapdragons, and Zinnias, are not "self-branching," but they can be encouraged to put out more branches and, therefore, more flowers by nipping off the top inch when the plants are four inches to six inches tall. I nip these plants in my garden in northern New Jersey only until the first week in July. If they are nipped too late in the growing season the flower buds have insufficient time to mature before the plant is struck by frost.

MORE FLOWERS will be encouraged to bloom, too, if you

keep the faded and dead flowers cut from the plants.

It may seem obvious but it bears repeating that for the maximum pleasure from your garden border the low plants should be planted to the front of the bed, the middle height plants behind them, and the tallest ones set across the back of the border: a theater of flower heads, so to speak.

POT GARDENING

Pot gardening is popular in Hong Kong where the fresh water supply is limited and much of the water used is bought from China. The restrictive use of water limits large-scale gardening and calls for plants that can survive the short water supply. The earth is often hard, brown, and dry, but walks, patios, and terraces are alive with splashes of the red and gold of plumed Celosia and the pink and magenta of Globe Amaranth, the favorite plants of Hong Kong's pot gardeners.

If your "garden" is a fire escape or a window box in a sunny situation, or if you live in a very dry climate with a limited water supply, try growing these Lazy Flowers in pots. Set one plant in a five-inch pot, or for a mass color effect set three plants in a larger pot. Celosia and Globe Amaranth are more than satisfactory in the color they provide, for once they begin to bloom their flowering is continuous. The blossoms do not "come and go" so quickly as do most other flowers but remain on the plant throughout the growing season, only very gradually going to seed. The color effect, then, is cumulative. As the plant grows and develops more spikes it develops more flowers, and, consequently, becomes both larger and more colorful as the growing season progresses.

Cut the stems of these Lazy Flowers near the base before they are nipped by Jack Frost, dry, and arrange, either by themselves or with other dried materials.

While pot gardening offers an opportunity for a bit of gardening in a dry climate where there might otherwise be none, it also offers an opportunity to place color in strategic places outdoors in almost any climate. The plants might be different from those preferred by Hong Kong's pot gardeners but whatever the choice try to select flowers which will provide continuous bloom throughout the growing season. Some of the More Effort Flowers that do well in pots (but not so well as the Celosia and Globe Amaranth in dry climates) are Geraniums, Calendulas, Zinnias, and the lower growing varieties of Marigolds.

Elizabeth Kent was probably the most enthusiastic pot gardener on record. Although she lived in London she was a country girl at heart, and country friends would often present her with potted plants as country mementos. Her initial efforts in behalf of their survival were disastrous until, finally, she "resolved to obtain and to communicate such information as should be requisite for the rearing and preserving a *portable garden* in pots." She recorded the results of her efforts in her book *Flora Domestica* in 1823. In her enthusiasm she appears to have developed the attitude that almost anything that would fit in a pot could be grown in a pot, and many a guest must have been startled to find Hollyhocks, Ox-Eye Daisies, and Honesty blooming in her "portable garden" in unexpected corners of her apartment. At varying seasons her pot garden produced colorful blossoms of Azalea, Hawthorn, Larkspur, Lavender, and Sea Lavender, to name but a few. These are all *Plant It Now, Dry It Later* plants, but few provide the continuous summer bloom which the annual plants give, and which is so desirable for porch or patio. However, with a little imagination and planning ahead you might startle and amuse your own guests on a special occasion with potted Hollyhocks blooming beside the front door or on the patio. Elizabeth Kent recommended that a one-foot-diameter pot be used for one Hollyhock plant, adding that the plant should be watered daily until it is well rooted.

If you have a garden and wish to try some of this imaginative pot gardening, plant the seed or plant in the appropriate size clay pot and sink the pot in the garden. This will eliminate special pot care of the plant until it comes into bloom. It will also eliminate the severe trauma a flowering plant undergoes when transplanted. At blooming time simply lift the pot and set it in its desired situation. Refer to the section "Flowers in the Order of Their Appearance in the Garden and along the Roadside" when selecting plants for specific booming times.

THE LOCAL FLORIST GARDEN

There is no need to feel excluded from the delights of flower drying simply because you have no garden and cannot plant it now. Many of the Lazy and More Effort Flowers and plant materials described in "Your Own Garden" are available from the local florist for drying and arranging, or simply arranging, at various times during the year.

Seasons come and go very quickly and it pays to anticipate which of the strictly seasonal flowers you might want to use at a later date to create your arrangements. This applies not only to the non-gardener but also to the gardener who finds he simply cannot grow all the plants he would like in his backyard or pot garden. Sometimes I find my own garden planning does not allow space for a favorite such as Statice, so I buy bunches in my favorite shades from the florist in February and March when it is in abundant supply rather than wait until fall when the supply is more limited. Acacia and Pussy Willow are other examples of seasonal materials which must be gathered early in the spring if there is any expectation of using them later.

The flower dryer who lives in an area of high humidity can take advantage of his florist in the fall and winter to supplement his Lazy Flower collection. And, of course, the florist can supply many flowers and materials not native to one's area: they supply me with the Ranunculus and Freesia of which I am so fond and would not otherwise have because they are difficult to grow in my garden, and others which grow not at all, such as Acacia and Eucalyptus.

The heart of the wholesale flower market on the East Coast is at the corner of 28th Street and Sixth Avenue

(Avenue of the Americas) in New York City. Here, within a block on each of the four points of the compass, trucks arrive to deliver their perishable cargo between four and six o'clock in the morning.

On a day in early spring trucks arrive from Florida laden with cartons of Statice and Anemone. Other trucks, making the last leg of air freight deliveries, converge on the busy intersection with Calendula, Ranunculus, Narcissus, and Heather from California, and Acacia (erroneously labeled "Mimosa") from Cannes in France.

As dawn breaks and shopkeepers set out on the curb their pails filled with Pussy Willow, branches of pink and white Peach Blossoms, Scotch Broom, Eucalyptus, and Forsythia, the gray streets and shabby buildings take on a festive air.

Empty shop windows become spectrums of color: the red, pink, purple, and white Anemones, pink Carnations, orange Calendulas, yellow, white, and blue Daisies, green Bells of Ireland, blue Bachelor's Buttons, yellow and lavender Statice, and mauve Heather, all interlaced with airy bunches of Baby's-Breath. These are among the *Plant It Now, Dry It Later* flowers that grace the wholesalers' windows in March. And it is from an exciting and wide variety such as this that your local florist selects the floral materials for his shop.

Obviously, it is impossible for your local florist to purchase *all* of the varieties of flowers available to him in the wholesale market. Quite likely, there are flowers which he himself prefers to work with, and these are the ones he is most likely to select. If you have in mind a particular kind that he does not normally buy, ask him to watch for it and to buy some for you.

With the arrival of crisp autumn air the dress of the wholesale flower market changes and most of the Lazy materials, those that have a strawlike quality or dry readily in air, become available. Strawflowers, plumed and crested Celosia, Teasel, Honesty, Chinese Lanterns, Bittersweet, Immortelle, Globe Amaranth, Yarrow, and Wood Roses make their appearance in the shop windows and in the shipping cartons along the curb. Also available are the colorful bunches of Skyrocket, a tiny starlike flower on a single stem. The latter are often dyed in beautiful [decorator] colors and can be used alone or arranged with other dried flowers. All of the materials in the arrangement on page 104 are available from your florist.

Many of the More Effort Flowers (those that are processed in silica gel) are available at the florist throughout the year. Just one word of caution when gathering these flowers for processing. Flowers from the florist are generally kept under refrigeration and contain considerable moisture, just as if they had been picked from the garden on a damp, humid day. Cut an inch from the stems and stand them in water for a few hours or overnight to allow this moisture to evaporate from the surface of the petals before processing.

There is rarely a storage problem when gathering flowers from the florist, for flowers are usually processed during the fall and winter months for immediate use. Perhaps you will decide that a mixed bouquet with Baby's-Breath as a filler material is just the arrangement for the coffee table for the winter.

Begin the arrangement by putting the Baby's-Breath, purchased fresh or dried in the fall, in the container selected. By itself it can be enjoyed for its light, airy appearance. Purchase and process one or a few flowers at a time (yellow and white Daisies, Roses, or Anemones as they become available), depending on the amount of silica gel you have. In this way you can select the color and size of each flower for your arrangement. As the flowers are dried add them to the Baby's-Breath. This "little by little" processing requires less silica gel, and each new flower will add a new dimension and fresh interest to the bouquet.

The florist is also your source of peacock and pheasant feathers, and the small materials needed to dry and arrange your flowers: the oasis, Posey Klay, florist's wire and florist's tape, and the desiccating medium, silica gel.

Where Some of the Flowers in My Local Florist
Garden Grow
I often gauge the soul of a city by whether or not flower
vendors are to be found on the street corners selling their
blooms when the weather permits, for what passerby is not
uplifted in spirit at the sight of bright blooms on an otherwise ordinary street?

One day in early April I found that San Francisco has a
soul. As I walked through the downtown area of the city I
spied the masses of bright flowers, and nostalgic memories
of the flower vendors of Paris and London swept over me.
The street corners were perfumed with the fragrance of
Gardenia, Lilac, Stock, and Sweet William; and the prized,
air-freighted flowers that I had left blooming indoors in my
Local Florist Garden at home were blooming madly in
buckets placed on sidewalk and stand. Pink, red, and
yellow Roses; pink and red Carnations; white, yellow, pink,
and blue Daisies; Tulips; and my favorites: pink Ranunculus and the deep purple Statice. Bunches of pink and
yellow Strawflowers hung from the perimeter of the roof of
the permanent sidewalk stand.

"All field grown within fifty miles of the city," said the
vendor proudly as he wrapped a large bunch of pink and red
Ranunculus which I had selected. If only my garden could
produce blooms like these!

A question or two determined that Monday, Wednesday,
and Friday are flower market days in San Francisco. The
three markets and twenty-two stores located on Brannan
Street between 5th and 6th Streets carry on an annual
volume of business which exceeds $25 million. It is one of
very few flower markets in the United States where the
grower sells directly to the trade. Between four and six
o'clock in the morning the flower growers drive their trucks
directly into the spacious buildings built to accommodate
them and unload their carefully wrapped blooms onto

rough tables from which they sell to the florists who begin to arrive in their trucks about five o'clock. I, too, arrived at that hour to wander through the buildings and enjoy the flowers and the people.

Most California flower growers specialize in one or two flowers, and it is no accident that their flowers are such perfect specimens. Soil testing, fertilizing, and spraying are as important to successful flower growing as they are to successful vegetable growing. And successful are the California flower growers! The buildings were a mass of pails filled with stately Gladiolus, giant Pacific Delphiniums, and perfect "football" Chrysanthemums. The Chrysanthemum grower sets out his plants every two weeks to keep his growing cycle going all year round.

I paused to visit with one grower who was unwrapping bright blue Carnations. "We have them in chartreuse, lavender, and peach colors, too," he replied to my inquiry regarding colors and dyeing. "They are dyed through the stem and cut twice during the sixteen-hour process. Quite different from the petal-dip dyeing of the blue Daisies."

On the next table were containers filled with (wouldn't you know?) Ranunculus and purple Statice. I stopped to admire the beautiful blooms. "Are you visiting?" the grower inquired pleasantly. When I replied that I was, he picked out two bunches of Ranunculus, wrapped them in a newspaper, and presented them to me. An unexpected and welcome gift!

That first week in April was near the end of his growing season, which extends from October 1 to about the end of March. "Do you know Freesias?" he asked. "I grow them, too." When asked if the flowers were grown nearby, he replied, "Yes, in Daly City. I grow them behind a mausoleum in a cemetery." Now, I have been in many commercial gardens in many places but never in one behind a mausoleum in a cemetery, and so I asked if I might visit. "Oh, yes," replied my friend, obviously pleased at an interest in his flowers. "Just find the lower gate to the cemetery and come right in to the top."

A few days later I drove to Daly City, which is just south of San Francisco, selected the proper cemetery from among those that line the highway, drove through the lower gate, on up to the top of the hill, and then to the back of the great mausoleum.

I was greeted by four or five acres of gardens which sloped gently upward from the rear of the mausoleum. The gardens were divided into large plots of about a half acre each. Each farmer was hoeing, watering, and otherwise tending his own half-acre garden. A woman bent over her neat mounds of Violets, picked a bunch of flowers and three leaves to form a small corsage, quickly wrapped a rubberband around the stems and tossed them into a basket. A few drops of water, and popped into a cellophane bag, and they, too, would be off to the San Francisco flower market.

Row upon row of Ranunculus covered the garden next to the Violets; Statice in all its gorgeous colors filled other plots, while mounds of white and yellow Daisies formed a frame for all. A charming and unusual commercial garden!

EVERYONE'S ROADSIDE GARDEN: PICK WITH CARE!

A discriminating look beyond your garden gate will identify many materials to add to your dried flower collection. Some of the wildflowers which grow in fields and by the wayside are beautiful when dried, and a keen eye can detect here and there a little gem that will provide a bonus for the dried bouquet. And, at times, gathering wildflowers can also test your ingenuity.

My own wildflower harvest began early and rather unexpectedly in April a few years ago when I was on a golfing holiday in South Carolina. I was fascinated by the huge rose and purple Thistles growing in the meadow adjacent to the golf course, and was determined to try drying a few. Inquiry provided the necessary permission to do some picking but if you have ever attempted to pick Thistles you know how impossible they are to grasp. The prickles of these great Thistles were in proportion to the size of the flowers—enormous! There was only one tool available that was adequate to the occasion, and I stood in the meadow practicing with my nine-iron, each stroke slicing clean through a Thistle stalk! The final effect was worth the effort, however, and the Thistle has become one of my favorite dried flowers. In my home state of New Jersey the Thistle flowers in August and early September. It is not nearly as large as its South Carolina cousin but it has greater depth of color.

When gathering wild flowers it is important to know which ones are useful to the dried bouquet and which are not; which ones may be picked freely without fear of causing their extinction, and which ones face extinction if picked. The latter deserve the best protective efforts of all of us if their beauty is to be left for future generations to enjoy.

Many states have found it necessary to enact legislation protecting some of their wild beauty from the extirpation which accompanies an advancing "civilization." Your state Agricultural Department can supply you with a list of the names of the plants that are protected by law. However, protective legislation for wild flowers is still in its infancy, and most states have provided protection only for those flowers and plants which would otherwise face early extinction. I am sure that concerned garden groups and botanists in almost every state have recommendations before their legislatures asking for protection of particular wild flowers whose survival is in jeopardy. These recommendations should be given early, and serious, consideration by all state legislators. In the last analysis, of course, it is not legislation that will save our vanishing natural beauty, but the concern of the people of our great nation for its survival. Legislation is important, but even more important is the education of our citizens to the importance of preserving living things.

Your state Agricultural Department may list wild plants in categories to denote their relative scarcity or abundance.

Such listings will provide some guidelines for your wild flower collecting.

For example, in New Jersey it is illegal to pick the following:

* Bittersweet
* Holly
Mountain Laurel

* Rhododendron
Winterberry
Ground Pine

Although legislation has not yet been extended to include the following, New Jersey pleads "Do Not Pick":

Partridge Berry
Pink Azalea
Rattlesnake Plantain
Cardinal Flower
Canada Lily

Wild Columbine
Pipsissewa
Pitcher Plant
Wild Philadelphia Lily

Labeled "Pick With Caution" are:

Spring Beauty
* Dog's-Tooth Violet
Bloodroot
Rue Anemone
Solomon's Seal
* Wild Geranium
Butterfly Weed
Wild Lily-of-the-Valley

Hepatica
Dutchman's Breeches
Wind Flower or Wood Anemone
Jack-in-the-Pulpit
False Solomon's Seal
Bellwort
Blue Lobelia
Marsh Marigold

Happily, you may "Pick Freely" in New Jersey:

* Queen Anne's Lace (Wild Carrot)
* Yarrow
* Daisy
* Aster
Joe-Pye Weed
* Dandelion
* Pearly Everlasting

Buttercup
* Black-Eyed Susan
* Goldenrod
Butter and Eggs
* Violet
* Ironweed
Wild Morning Glory

And, of course, the Thistle, Sea Lavender, and Reed Grass, too common for even this last category, must not be overlooked, and are yours for the lawful picking.

The need for protective legislation to save our wild plants is well illustrated by Wake Robin *(Trillium)*, an

---

*These are the plant materials recommended for the dried bouquet. Those in the "Illegal" category are recommended for home garden planting, leaving the wild specimens for all to enjoy.

exquisite flower that appears on the "Don't Pick" list in virtually every state in which it is found. It is only one of many wild flowers deserving of our concern, but its story serves as a good example of why many of our native plants, if disturbed, face extinction, and why these flowers should never be picked for the momentary pleasure they might give.

When grown from seed the *Trillium* plant is five or six years old before it produces its first flower which appears, early in the spring, immediately above three leaves on a stem. Below ground during those years, the seed has developed into a bulb which is dependent upon those same three leaves to manufacture the food essential to its growth. When picked, the stem is invariably cut or broken below the leaves. The picker, then, not only eliminates the possibility of reproduction of the *Trillium* by seed propagation—a lengthy process at best—but also robs the remaining bulb of the nourishment it needs to survive and to produce a flower the following year.

Another plant rapidly being added to the "Don't Pick" lists is Bittersweet. This climbing vine, whose showy red and orange berries add color to the fall and winter landscape, is fast disappearing because of the ruthless cutting and tearing of those who sell the colorful sprays for indoor decoration. Michigan law prohibits the picking of this lovely wild vine, and Connecticut protects Bittersweet because of its value as game food. Planting in your garden the improved varieties of Bittersweet that are available from nurserymen will enable you to enjoy this colorful fall vine, and aid in its conservation, too.

The Indians knew the importance of plant conservation and reproduction to maintain food supplies for themselves and for animals. While our concern today is not so much to maintain a food supply for ourselves, the rules of the Indians still apply:

1. Take only as much as you need
2. Always leave a seed stock

3. Do not destroy the whole (the plant) in order to obtain a part (the blossom)
4. Observe the rights of another's hunting ground (property)

Our rules today are more formally stated in state laws which not only protect plants but also prohibit trespassing on private property to collect flowers from plants and trees. Most states also forbid picking along public highways and on public lands.

To sum up, the roadside garden, whether it is literally along a roadside or in the fields, woods, bogs, or marshes, is for everyone's *visual* pleasure, so whenever you gather from this garden be a lawful picker both in *where* you pick and in *what* you pick. Cut the stems carefully and the plants will provide you and others with their beauty year after year.

TURN YOUR ATTENTION TO THOSE CHARMING ROADSIDE FLOWERS —THE WEEDS!

All aspects of nature are interrelated, and as man has changed his own community and the use of the land he has affected the other natural communities around him. Virgin forests have fallen to the lumberman's ax; wildflowers have fallen prey to grazing and agriculture, and to the advance of the cities and the highways which accompany them. There has been a rise in the use of herbicides in an effort to kill off weeds such as Thistle, the bane of the agriculturist. Unfortunately, herbicides do not distinguish between the culprits and the innocents, and as a result much of our wild beauty is being sprayed out of existence.

Some of the so-called weeds are among the most useful flowers for the dried bouquet. Actually, some charming roadside flowers, such as the Ox-Eye Daisy, Queen Anne's Lace, Tansy, and Pearly Everlasting, were introduced into America from Europe as cultivated specimens in the gardens of early settlers. Evidently the climate and soil conditions more than agreed with them and they escaped under early garden fences to create a population explosion across much of the United States. They have been better able to adjust to the incursions of human activity than many of our native wildflowers, and are often found flourishing in recently disturbed roadside beds and in newly plowed fields where their unwelcome presence has earned them the unflattering title of "weeds." In their abundance these early garden treasures are all but ignored.

It is a characteristic of human nature to consider beautiful whatever is rare simply because of its rarity. We tend to overlook the more common flowers simply because they are so common. But look carefully at Queen Anne's Lace or the Ox-Eye Daisies when next they are in flower—as if you were seeing them for the first time. If they were rare, would they not be prized in anyone's garden?

The following are the weeds which I have found to be most useful to the colorful dried bouquet, and some of the states in which they can legally be picked freely. (This is not to say that they may not be picked freely elsewhere, but that most other states have not yet so classified their wild plants.)

Yarrow
Arkansas
Indiana
New Jersey
Pennsylvania
Virginia
West Virginia
Wisconsin

Aster
Arkansas
Illinois
Indiana
New Jersey
North Carolina
Pennsylvania
West Virginia

Cattail
Indiana
West Virginia

Thistle
Arkansas
Indiana
New Jersey
Pennsylvania
Virginia
Wisconsin

Ironweed
Arkansas
Indiana
North Carolina
Pennsylvania
Kansas
West Virginia

Queen Anne's Lace
Arkansas
Indiana
New Jersey
North Carolina
Pennsylvania
Virginia
West Virginia
Wisconsin

Tansy
Arkansas
Indiana
Wisconsin

Ox-Eye Daisy
Arkansas
Indiana
New Jersey
North Carolina
Pennsylvania
Virginia
West Virginia
Wisconsin

Goldenrod
Arkansas
Indiana
New Jersey

North Carolina
Pennsylvania
Virginia
Kansas
West Virginia

Black-Eyed Susan
Arkansas
New Jersey
North Carolina
Pennsylvania
Virginia
West Virginia
Wisconsin

I confine my own wayside flower collecting to plants listed under "Pick Freely." The trees I have recommended for their flowers or foliage, such as Dogwood, Redbud, Hawthorn, and Holly, which fall into the protected categories when found in the woodlands, are in my own garden, as are Pussy Willow and Rhododendron. They are, therefore, available for careful cutting.

The wildflowers and plants which appear on the "Don't Pick" lists but which dry well, such as Wild Geranium, Lenten Rose, Dog's-Tooth Violet, Maidenhair Fern, and May Apple, have been gathered from the wildflower gardens of friends. You, too, may be inspired to set aside a shady corner of the garden for some of these wild beauties. If so, don't try to plant a corner of your garden with native plants from the woodlands.

Attempts to transplant rare varieties of native flowers from their natural habitat to the home garden are rarely successful. Soil, moisture, and shade are among the ecological factors which are crucial to their survival, and these can seldom be duplicated.

In developing your own wildflower garden it is far better to purchase your plants from reliable nurserymen who specialize in wildflower culture and propagation. The varieties which they offer are those which are most likely to acclimate themselves best to a "cultivated" wildflower garden. In this way you will be able to enjoy the rarer wild beauties and practice conservation, too. Your local nurseryman can identify growers from whom wild plants may be purchased.

As you develop a sense of awareness of what is growing in the fields and along the roadside you, too, will have a new appreciation of the colorful treasures of the earth. You will also realize how rapidly earthmovers and tractors are destroying them, and so your wildflower gardening takes on a new importance—as a means of preserving the flora native to your area.

I find that I eagerly anticipate finding the wild plants suitable for use in the dried bouquet blooming in their old familiar places as the growing season progresses. With just a little practice an inquiring eye will find the Pussy Willow in March, the Dogwood, May Apple, and Wild Geranium in May (these in the gardens of friends), Wheat and Yarrow in June; the Black-Eyed Susans, Ironweed, and Queen Anne's Lace in July; Thistles, Tansy, Reed Grass, and Goldenrod in August, and the Cattails and Pearly Everlasting in September. And it is with increasing frequency that I am disappointed to find that in the name of "progress" a favorite patch of Goldenrod has been replaced by another factory or highway.

Wildflowers processed in silica gel—Wild Geranium and Black-Eyed Susan, for example—tend to droop quite readily after they are picked. If it is possible to carry some water to put them in immediately after picking, by all means do so. If not, cut an inch from the stems when you get home and stand them in water overnight for processing the next day. If their fresh firmness has not been restored and they are still droopy, you might well discard them, for the dried flower can never look fresher than the fresh flower appeared before processing.

Dry It Later

How To Dry
the Lazy Flowers

The Lazy Flowers and plant materials are those which require *little* or *no processing* after they have been cut.

Actually, the flower heads and seed pods of most of the Lazy materials are already dry when cut, and the difference between little processing and no processing is really a matter of drying the Lazy Flower *stems,* rather than the flowers themselves.

Some of the Lazy Flowers and Fruits, such as Cattail, Sea Lavender, and Japanese Bamboo, have stiff or woody stems which retain their stiffness after cutting. They require no processing, and can be arranged immediately after cutting.

Other Lazy Flowers, such as Globe Amaranth, Winged Everlasting, and Statice, have soft stems, and to arrange them immediately after cutting would be to encourage them to hang their heads. So that these flowers will present their best appearance in the dried bouquet their soft stems must first be given time to dry and harden. I bundle together five or six stems of the same flower with string or fine wire and tie the bundles to a wire coat hanger which I hang in the basement, attic, a closet, or other dark place. The drying and hardening time for stems averages about two weeks; it varies slightly, depending on the plant and the humidity.

Drying some of the Lazy Flowers

The Strawflower is the one Lazy Flower that merits special attention. Because of the tendency of these flowers to blossom singly and sequentially along the stem, the maximum number of blooms will be gathered from a plant

1. Ground Pine
2. Summer Salvia
3. Statice, purple
4. Japanese Bamboo
5. Plumed Celosia
6. Lavender
7. Ornamental Corn
8. Baby's Breath
9. Teasel
10. Reed Grass
11. Sea Lavender
12. Globe Amaranth, magenta
13. Rhodanthe, rose
14. Globe Amaranth, pink
15. Wood Rose
16. Strawflowers
17. Rhodanthe, yellow
18. Immortelle
19. Statice, yellow
20. Acacia
21. Ammobium
22. Pussy Willow
23. Honesty
24. Pussy Toes
25. Globe Thistle
26. Statice White

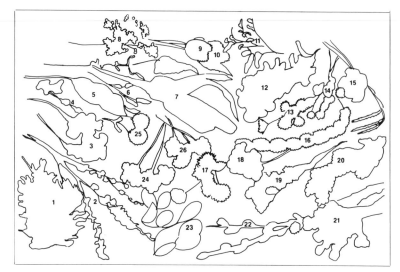

An assortment of Lazy Flowers (Figure 5)

if the flowers are picked one at a time and a wire stem is substituted for the natural stem when the flower is first picked and both stem and flower are soft and easily pierced. The wire may be attached in one of two ways: Either thread the wire into the short natural stem and push it up into the flower, taking care not to break through its face, and hang or stand it aside to allow the natural stem to dry and harden. Or simply pierce the wire into the back of the flower adjacent to the natural stem—a less time-consuming method used by commercial florists.

A rather whimsical way to handle Strawflowers which may appeal to you as much as it does to me is to wire the flowers in sprays to give the effect in Fig. 5. To do this I lay aside several lengths of wire on which I string the flowers, like beads, from a few plants during the growing season. The best effect is obtained when the flowers are graduated in size. The flowers will slip about on the wire at first but as they dry and harden they become firmly positioned. Make any final adjustment in the position of the flower *before* it hardens in place.

If you buy your Strawflowers already wired instead of growing your own, the same effect can be achieved by using florist's tape to bind the wire stems together, bending the wires at the flower heads so that all the heads are turned in the same direction.

To create a spray of Strawflowers (top), either string the flowers on a wire (center), or bind together their wire stems (bottom)

How To Dry the More Effort Flowers

Through the years I have used a variety of desiccating materials to preserve flowers: fine, washed, and throughly dried sand; or a mixture of sand and borax; or ⅓ cup borax to each ⅔ cup of white cornmeal. Although the results were satisfactory, they did not begin to compare with those achieved when silica gel was substituted as the desiccant. Actually not a "gel" at all, silica gel is a dry, granular, nontoxic substance that looks like sugar or table salt. I prefer it to other desiccating mediums for the following reasons:

1. In the time-conscious era we live in it is far more gratifying to see the results of one's flower-drying efforts in two to seven days than to wait out the two to three weeks required to process flowers in sand or other media. This shorter drying time becomes very important if my technique is faulty and a lopsided flower emerges from the silica gel. After only a few days I can usually find another flower of its kind still in bloom in the garden and try again, but by the time a faulty Tulip or Peony emerges from two or more weeks in sand those flowers have passed their prime for drying and my collection is the poorer for lack of them.

2. For the same volume of desiccating medium I am able to process many more flowers with silica gel. Putting it another way, to dry a given number of flowers far more sand is needed than silica gel, and additional storage space must be provided for the sand during the longer processing period.

 1. Peony, Herbaceous
 2. Bell Flower
 3. Crocus, Autumn Flowering
 4. Azalea
 5. Rose
 6. Rose
 7. Rose, Polyantha: "The Fairy"
 8. Zinnia
 9. Rose, "Betty Prior"
10. Larkspur
11. Rose
12. Pansy
13. Johnny-Jump-Up
14. Freesia
15. Dogwood
16. Day Lily
17. Marigold, Yellow
18. Daffodil
19. Bells of Ireland
20. Marigold, Orange
21. Black-Eyed Susan
22. Chrysanthemum, "Charles Nye"
23. Primrose
24. Maidenhair Fern
25. Snapdragon
26. Anemone
27. Stokesia
28. Dahlia, Pom-Pom
29. Anemone
30. Geranium
31. Tulip
32. Shasta Daisy
33. Bridal Wreath
34. Dahlia
35. Sunflower
36. Hollyhock
37. Peony, Tree

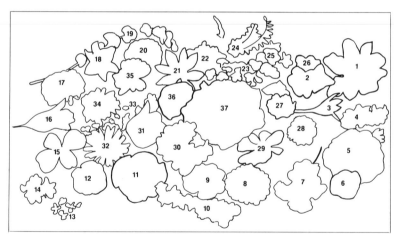

A Selection of More Effort Flowers (Figure 6)

As an industrial desiccating agent, silica gel is commercially available under several trade names and in many sizes of granules, most of which are too large to be useful in drying flowers. If you purchase your silica gel from a chemical supply company where it is available in one-, five-, and twenty-five-pound quantities, request "mesh 28-200," a granule size that processes flowers well yet is not so fine that it is prohibitive in cost. The Plant-Tabs Corporation of Timonium, Maryland, packages the desiccant in one-and-a-half-, four-, and twenty-pound tins under the name "Flower-Dri," which is sold by many garden centers and florists and hobby shops. Flower-Dri has an added advantage because it contains "tel-tale" granules which act as a built-in moisture absorption indicator. These tel-tale granules are bright blue when the silica gel is dry and its moisture-absorbing ability is at a maximum. As you use it once, twice, and three times the blue color fades, indicating a growing moisture content, and then finally turns pale pink when the silica gel is saturated. These indicators are important because your silica gel will feel dry to the touch whether it is new and unused or saturated with moisture.

"Keep your powder dry!" was the cry of the artilleryman of another day, and it might well be the byword of the flower dryer. Though silica gel is not strictly speaking a powder, your success with drying flowers in this or any other desiccating medium depends on its ability to absorb the total moisture from the flower. When the silica gel has absorbed its full moisture capacity it must be reactivated, or dried out, before it can be successfully used again. There is no limit to the number of times the silica gel can be reactivated or how many times it can be used. Simply put your tin of silica gel in a 275–300° oven for fifteen or twenty minutes, or for quicker drying spread it on a cookie sheet. To aid the drying process, I stir the gel once with a slotted spoon to bring the bottom granules to the surface. You will find that the pink tel-tale granules will return to their

HOW TO DRY
FLOWERS IN SILICA
GEL

bright blue hue as the silica gel dries out. Replace the lid immediately after removing the tin from the oven. Allow the silica gel to cool before using. If it is used while it is still warm it tends to "burn" petals and discolor them slightly.

I find I can use my silica gel four or five times before reactivating it when drying flowers in tins. There are exceptions, of course, and I pop the silica gel into the oven after each drying of Marigolds, Asters, Chrysanthemums, and a few other flowers which require five to seven days for processing. It is also wise to reactivate it after using the open method of drying recommended for flowers with sturdy stems, for the silica gel absorbs moisture not only from the flower but also from the surrounding air.

SELECTING THE FLOWERS

The list of flowers and plant materials that can be processed successfully in silica gel is long and still growing, and quite likely you may wish to experiment with some of your own favorites that are not discussed in this book. A few words about some basic principles of flower drying and one or two "don't bother to try these" should keep the beginner from experiencing failure and disappointment with his (or her) early efforts.

Flowers to be processed in silica gel should be selected for their form, the firmness of their petals and, most important, the stage of their development. Generally, the flowers that dry best are those like the Daisy and Rose that have bladelike petals which can be surrounded, top and bottom, by the silica gel. I avoid drying flowers with sac-shaped petals (for example Wisteria, Bleeding Heart, Lupine, and Thermopsis) because of the "air space" between the two surfaces. Unless this air space can be filled with the desiccant (a difficult and arduous task), the flowers become flattened and misshapen during the processing. My own feeling is that this is hardly worth the effort when so many

Bleeding Heart

flowers dry so beautifully without special treatment.

When selecting flowers for drying, I choose varieties with flatter petals. For instance, the Cactus-petaled varieties of Zinnias and Dahlias do not process as well as their flatter-petaled counterparts because of the difficulty of slipping the silica gel under their tightly curled edges. When selecting Snapdragons for drying I choose the newer Bellflower and Butterfly varieties because their single flowers are more open and easier to fill with silica gel than the flowers of the older kinds.

Do not overlook the more modest yields of the garden. A small Zinnia, cheerful in color and well-formed, may not be the prize of your outdoor efforts, but indoors, in winter, this same small flower will take on a new importance.

Always process a few more flowers than you expect to use. Not all of your drying results are sure to please, and allowance must be made, too, in the event that an accident or mishandling causes a shattering of petals.

Form. Nature has her flaws, as we well know, so when selecting flowers for processing choose those with the fewest flaws, for while processing can capture the transient beauty of the flower it cannot *improve* its form or appearance.

Petal Firmness. The petals of flowers selected for processing should be fresh and firm to the touch. If the petals appear droopy from lack of water cut an inch from the stems and stand the flowers in water until their fresh appearance has been restored. Flowers with petals droopy from old age should be discarded.

Timing is perhaps the most important factor in successful flower drying. And timing refers to the stage of development of the flower when it is picked for processing. If it is picked too early in its development it will not provide its full beauty; if it is picked beyond the peak of its maturity it will tend to deteriorate and break apart during the drying process. Experience, as elsewhere, proves to be the best teacher, and the flower dryer soon learns that the optimum picking time for success in drying is when each flower *approaches* its peak of bloom. But the dried bouquet will gain added interest if some of the flowers are captured at earlier stages of development: the unopened bud, or one which is only slightly opened, or a flower that has not attained its full size will all add a pleasing measure of proportion and variety of form to the bouquet.

All Flowers Must Be Surface-Dry Before Processing if the very best results are to be achieved, so pick your flowers in the late morning when the dew has evaporated from the petals. If they cannot be processed immediately, stand them in water to retain the petal firmness. This is necessary, too, for flowers that must be picked while they are still heavy with dew, and for those plucked from the first drops of an oncoming storm.

TECHNIQUES OF DRYING FLOWERS IN SILICA GEL

Success with drying flowers is mostly a matter of technique—and a little patience. The technique is easy to develop and certainly the little patience needed is far less than the patience required for other kinds of art work. I know no other way to achieve so much decorative beauty with so little effort. Paintings and tapestries may last longer, but the beauty and variety of real flowers, whether they are fresh or dried, can never be equalled.

Everyone who dries flowers gradually develops his or her own successful techniques. My own are adapted to three basic flower forms:

1. The single flower (Daisy, Rose, Sunflower).
2. Stalks of flowers (Delphinium, Larkspur, Stock, Bells of Ireland).
3. Flower clusters on sturdy stems (Globe Thistle, Hydrangea, Queen Anne's Lace, Feverfew).

The exceptions are a few flower clusters on not-so-sturdy stems, such as Verbena, Primula, annual Baby's-Breath, Geranium, and Phlox. These I wire and dry as if they were single flowers.

Whichever flower form you are working with, careful attention to these three points will help you achieve success:

1. Make every effort to retain the three-dimensional appearance of the flower when applying the silica gel.
2. *Curb your curiosity.* Don't peek until the processing has been completed.
3. *Spill* the silica gel off the flowers when the processing has been completed. *Do not pull* the flowers out of the desiccant.

CONTAINERS FOR PROCESSING

Flowers may be dried in a variety of containers. Tins with tight-fitting lids are best and range from the one-pound shortening tin, good for a single Rose, to the larger fruitcake tin, which can accommodate a variety of flowers.

Shoeboxes and florist boxes may be used to dry Bells of Ireland, Larkspur, Delphinium, and other materials whose length cannot be accommodated in round tins. Inasmuch as silica gel absorbs moisture from all of its surroundings, it is important to dry flowers in boxes when the humidity is low—a rule which also applies when processing flowers on sturdy stems in tall, open tins.

Flowers which have similar drying periods should be processed together to make the most economical use of your silica gel.

THE SINGLE FLOWER

If you have never dried flowers in a desiccating medium, try first some simple single flowers—the Daisy or the Sunflower—before launching into those which require more refined techniques, such as the Crocus and Tulip. Buy a few Daisies from the florist to develop your own technique before the growing season begins. Botanically speaking, the Daisy and the Sunflower are not single flowers. Each is composed of a flower cluster surrounded by rays. However, for drying purposes, they have been classified as single flowers. They are classic examples of simplicity and beginning with the easiest will give you an opportunity to wire the flower, work with the silica gel, be "all thumbs," and still achieve moderate success. By the time the Crocus and the Tulips are in flower you should have developed sufficient confidence and proficiency to achieve success in drying those early spring beauties.

The final appearance of single flowers will be most natural if they are processed face-up in the silica gel rather than face down. I prefer to wire each flower—that is, to replace the natural stem with a wire one—before drying. Wiring is a simple procedure and once wired, the flower is easier to handle in drying, storing, and particularly in arranging, for the bendable wire enables the flower head to assume any angle in the arrangement without appearing stiff.

HOW TO WIRE SINGLE FLOWERS

Cut a three-to-four-inch length of wire from your #23 wire spool. The length of the wire is not important, for it can be cut or added to when the arrangement is made; what *is* important is that the natural stem, which becomes rigid when dry, is replaced with a flexible one (the wire) while the flower is fresh and soft and easily pierced. Attempts to wire flower heads after they are dry and hard can be frustrating and often result in broken flowers, so for best results wire them before processing.

A point to remember: When handling wired flowers *always apply pressure to the wire,* not to the flower or to its natural stem.

1. Cut all but ¾ of an inch from the flower stem. Run the wire up into the remaining stem. The wire may be pushed through the base of the calyx, but do not permit it

Wiring the single flower (1)

to show through the face of the flower. As the stem dries it shrinks and hardens and forms a firm bond with the wire. Although this is my preferred method of wiring and applies to most flowers, two other methods are worth noting because of their adaptability to particular flowers:

2. Zinneas have large, hollow stems and may be wired in this manner: The wire should be run up through the stem and driven through the urn-shaped receptacle and out the face of the flower. Bend this end of the wire one-half inch back along itself (180°) and pull gently on the other end of the wire to hook the bent end into the flower face.

3. Flowers like Marigolds with a large, hollow stem and a very heavy base may be wired in another way: Pass the wire horizontally through the receptacle, extending it about an inch and a half beyond. Bend the wire on either side of the calyx down along the stem, and twist.

(2)

HOW TO RETAIN THE NATURAL APPEARANCE OF FRESH FLOWERS

The final form of the dried flower will be determined by its position when it is surrounded by silica gel. The silica gel holds the flower firmly in place while it quickly absorbs its moisture. Some people are disappointed in the final result because the flowers emerge from the desiccant flat or misshapen. A flat appearance is the result of *dumping* the silica gel on the flower rather than *sprinkling* it so as to provide support for the flower petals before covering them. A little patience and care, then, are needed in applying the silica gel.

Spread some newspaper where you are going to work to retrieve any spilled granules of silica gel. I store my silica gel in the tins in which I do the processing, so I must spill some out before I begin to work. A small, flexible plastic basin is convenient for spilling the silica gel from one container to another.

Spill all but three-fourths inch of the desiccant from the tin, and then hold up the wire stem of the flower to be dried. In positioning the flower in silica gel it is important to cater as much as possible to the natural grace of the flower. If the petals have a naturally droopy appearance (as Black-Eyed Susans sometimes do), hill up a little extra silica gel where the flower is to be placed so that the petals can droop in the silica gel during the drying process. Bend the wire stem where it enters the natural stem, remembering to apply the pressure to the wire, not to the flower itself. If several flowers are to be dried in a single tin allow about one inch between them. To best preserve the form of the flower, spill the desiccant down the sides of the container *away* from the flower. As the silica gel slides down it slips under the petals, giving them support before they are covered. This method prevents the flat, unnatural appearance which dried flowers sometimes have. Continue to add the silica gel in this manner, sprinkling a little over the top of the flower until it is completely covered. Strike the side of the tin a few times to settle the desiccant well into the center of the flower, and cover any petal tips that might have become exposed by the striking. Secure the lid firmly in place and set the tin aside for the specified drying time. I find it convenient to note on the top of the tin, either on a strip of masking tape or a piece of paper taped to the lid, the contents and the date and time that their processing will be completed. If you have many tins of many flowers all drying at the same time, imagine the confusion which could arise if their unseen contents are unidentified!

Adding the silica gel

DRYING THE FAVORITE SINGLE FLOWER: THE ROSE.

Gather ye Rosebuds while ye may.
Old time is still a-flying
And this same flower that smiles today,
Tomorrow will be dying.

Herrick was not referring to real flowers when he wrote his "Hesperides," but I daresay he might be surprised to find that the real Rosebud that smiles in the garden today can still be smiling many months hence if it is processed in silica gel. The transient beauty of the Rose can be captured—from the bud to the more open flower—if the petals are firm and have not begun to fade. The technique is a little more refined for Roses that are picked at more open stages of development, so begin with the slightly opened buds.

Roses may be dried in various stages of development

Wire the stem, using Method 1. Put three-fourths inch of silica gel in the tin. Hill up another one-quarter to one-half inch where the Rose is to be positioned. Holding the outer petals, gently but firmly press the Rose into the silica hill, which will give support at the base of the outer petals. Gradually add the crystals, taking care to sprinkle some between the petals. For a more open Rose, support must be provided for the outer petals first, the second tier of petals next, and so on, gradually working the silica gel over the outer petals and toward the center of the flower until it is completely covered. Strike the tin, cover the tips of any exposed petals, and set aside for four or five days. More open Roses should be left in the silica gel for the full processing period to assure the hardening of all parts of the flower and the firm positioning of its petals. Occasionally, if I am hard pressed to recover the desiccant to dry other flowers, I remove slightly opened Roses after only two days, at which time the outer petals are dry to the touch but the deep center of the flower and the calyx are soft and still contain considerable moisture; quite likely, the petals will not be firm in their position. The drying and hardening process will continue in air, although the time required for all parts to become thoroughly dry will be somewhat longer than if the drying had been completed in the desiccant. Bend the end of the wire stem and loop it over a wire hanger to permit the Rose to hang upside down while the drying process is completed. This deep drying can take a few days to a week, depending on the size of the Rose and the humidity of the air. Often I will hang a Rose for a day or two and then stand it face up to permit the outer petals to fall back a bit and give the flower a more open appearance.

A bit of melted paraffin at the base will give these outer petals added support. This is a matter of judgment and experience, so experiment a bit to achieve the effect you like best.

PROCESSING SINGLE FLOWERS THAT ARE CUPLIKE IN FORM.

Rose of Sharon, Platycodon, Crocus, and Tulip—like the Rose, these flowers must first be supported around the outer base of the petals. Then add the silica gel, sprinkling some inside, some outside, continuing in this manner gradually to build up the level of the silica gel inside and outside the petals so they are neither pushed in nor out by uneven distribution of the dessicant.

STALKS AND SPRAYS OF FLOWERS (DELPHINIUM, LARKSPUR, STOCK, BELLS OF IRELAND, ETC.)

Drying a stalk of flowers: Stock

Select a container that most nearly approximates the shape and size of the spray to be dried. A shoebox is usually sufficient for all but the tall Delphinium, which may require a larger florist's box to accommodate its length. When using boxes it is generally wise to reinforce all edges and corners with masking tape to prevent any loss of silica gel through cracks or crevices.

Put one-fourth to one-half inch of silica gel in the bottom of the box. Cut two or three pieces of lightweight cardboard as shown and stand them in the silica gel along the length of the box as seen at left. These will serve as supports for the stalk or stem and will allow the single flowers on the bottom side of the stalk to retain a natural position during the drying process. Press the cut end of the stalk down into the silica gel and add the remaining desiccant as described on page 83.

FLOWER CLUSTERS ON STURDY STEMS (GLOBE THISTLE, HYDRANGEA, QUEEN ANNE'S LACE, FEVERFEW, ETC.)

The stiff stems and clustered growth of some flowers make it practical to dry them upside-down in the desiccant. It is best to use this method when the weather is clear and the humidity is low because the flowers remain on the stems and the container is uncovered throughout the drying process.

Put one-half inch of silica gel in the bottom of a tall container, the sides of which will provide support for the long stems. The five-pound tin in which the silica gel is sold serves very well, but any open-mouthed tall container will do.

Hold the flower upside down so that it rests gently on the surface of the desiccant. Gently spoon silica gel down the sides of the container until the flower or spray is covered. In the case of sprays such as Feverfew, only the tallest flower will rest on the silica gel at first. As that one is covered and the level of the silica gel rises each flower in turn will rest on, and then be surrounded and covered by, the silica gel.

To spill the silica gel off the flowers when the processing has been completed: Tip the tin or box to allow the silica gel to spill slowly into a basin or empty tin. As the flower and its wire stem begin to appear grasp the wire with one hand *to provide support only*—do not pull!—and continue to spill the silica gel until the flower is free from the desiccant. For flowers with sturdy stems: Provide support for the flowers by grasping the stem *before* beginning to spill the silica gel, continuing this support until the flower is free. To remove excess granules of silica gel from the processed flowers: Hold the wire or natural stem in your left hand and tap the stem near the flower head gently with a pencil or finger. Petals may be further groomed by brushing them carefully with a sable artists' brush to remove any remaining granules of silica gel.

Drying a flower cluster on a sturdy stem: Queen Anne's Lace

Spilling the silica gel from Sunflowers

Most flowers processed in silica gel retain their color beautifully through the drying process. A few undergo a slight color change, but, after experimenting with some ninety different flowers, I find there seems to be no basis for a general rule except to say that whatever color changes do take place seem to involve the reds, and then not all of those.

There is virtually no change in the color of yellow, orange, blue, and white flowers, or the green Bells of

COLOR CHANGES OF FLOWERS DRIED IN SILICA GEL

Ireland. The pinks of Roses are relatively free from color change, but the deep reds turn an unattractive brown, and I avoid drying them. The pink to deep rose Peonies, both herbaceous and tree, remain true at every shade. The rosy pinks of Zinnias darken just a bit, but deep red Zinnias, like Roses, dry a disappointing brown. The pinks and reds of Geraniums are just as cheery when they emerge from the silica gel as they were before processing, and the bright red of the Wiek single-bedding Dahlia, while dulling slightly, is still very pretty. The lavender of the Aster and Verbena become beautiful shades of blue, but the lavender of Scabiosa, Thistle, and Larkspur undergo no change in color.

Foliage

Plant It Now, Dry It Later arrangements may be created with the addition of sprays of leaves such as the Beech and Eucalyptus, in Fig. 11, or with single leaves such as the Hardy Cyclamen in Fig. 14; they may make use of the whimsical velvet leaves seen in the arrangement in Fig. 13, or they may be created with no leaves at all! Even if your anticipated needs for fall and winter dried flower arranging do not include foliage, it is wise to process a few leaves during the growing season so they will be available during the winter months should your needs change. There is nothing so rare as a spray of Beech leaves in December, and it is curiously gratifying to find in my *hortus siccus* these soft, supple leaves, and those of the Flowering Crabapple and Purple Plum, whose trees outdoors have long since given up their leaves to winter.

Some foliage for drying is gathered from deciduous trees and shrubs, others from evergreens, and still others from herbaceous plants during the summer months. In contrast, the leaves of the Hardy Cyclamen appear in late summer and are available for processing during the fall and winter.

With the exception of sprays of Eucalyptus and Ground Pine brought from my florist, and oddities such as Passion-flower leaves which live in local greenhouses, all of the foliage I use for drying grows in my garden in northern New Jersey. Undoubtedly, there are leaves from many other plants that can be preserved successfully, and you may wish to experiment with favorites of your own that are not included here. When doing so, select those leaves that are attractive and decorative to contribute the most beauty to your dried bouquet.

The foliage selected will respond readily to simple processing:

1. In a solution of glycerin and water
2. In silica gel, or
3. By hanging

For centuries pressing flowers and leaves between sheets of paper has been a popular way to preserve these botanical materials. However, I have omitted pressing as a method of preserving flowers and foliage because their final appearance lacks a three-dimensional quality consistent with the efforts of *Plant It Now, Dry It Later.*

The types of foliage which are included for your planting and drying pleasure are those which are simple to process, easy to work with, and will provide the most graceful and satisfactory appearance in the dried bouquet. Some, such as Eucalyptus and Ivy, will be familiar to the fresh flower arranger, while others, such as Pear and Devilwood, contribute different forms to the dried bouquet. Some of those that are processed in glycerin and water undergo color changes during the processing which adds a new dimension to their appearance and to your arranging.

PROCESSING FOLIAGE IN GLYCERIN AND WATER	*FOLIAGE*	*COLOR AFTER PROCESSING*
	Azalea, evergreen *(Rhododendron* spp*)*	olive green
	Beech, Silver, Other Beeches *(Fagus* spp*)*	green or other colors, depending on the kind of Beech
	Boxwood *(Buxus japonica)*	green
	Bull Bay *(Magnolia grandiflora)*	chocolate brown
	Devilwood *(Osmanthus americanus)*	olive green
	Dogwood *(Cornus florida)*	green during summer; autumn tones in fall
	Flowering Crabapple *(Malus sp)*	bronze-toned green
	Holly *(Ilex opaca)*	olive green

Ivy *(Hedera helix)*	olive green
Juniper *(Juniperus communis var. depressa)*	green
Lilac *(Syringa* spp)	brownish-bronze
Lily-of-the-Valley Tree *(Oxydendron arboreum)*	tawny gold in summer; autumn tones in fall
Mountain Laurel *(Kalmia latifolia)*	bronzy-green
Oregon Holly Grape *(Mahonia aquifolium)*	grayish-green
Pin Oak *(Quercus palustris)*	autumn tones in fall
Pear *(Pyrus communis)*	bronzy-brown
Purple Plum *(Prunus cerasifera var. pissardii)*	purple
Rhododendron *(Rhododendron* spp)	bronzy-green
Silver Dollar Tree/Eucalyptus *(Eucalyptus cinerea)*	silver green or mahogany red

HOW TO PROCESS IT

Prepare your solution of glycerin and water *before* cutting the branches. Cut ends of branchlets should be submerged *immediately after cutting* to permit maximum absorption of the solution. Branches should never be placed in water alone before processing as this retards the ability of the leaves to absorb the solution, often with disappointing results. The processing steps are very simple:

1. Choose a tall, thin jar, rather than a short, squat one, for processing. A quart mason jar is adequate for six to eight sprays of leaves. Fill the jar with a solution of ⅓ glycerin and ⅔ warm water. Stir.
2. Select sprays and branches with the most perfect leaves to assure the best appearance in your bouquet. Remember that while processing preserves the leaves it cannot improve on their appearance. Leaves that are tattered and perforated before processing are still tattered and perforated after processing, so select your leaves carefully. I prefer to pick leaves for processing during July and August

when the new growth has matured and before the
leaves have deteriorated due to wind, rain, and
insects. If the only leaves available have slightly
rough edges process those and trim them later to
improve their appearance. (See "Repairs and Reinforcements," page 114.) Sprays of leaves up to
eighteen to twenty inches in length will absorb the
glycerin and water successfully.

3. With a hammer pound the bottom four to five
   inches of the branch, leaving it in a chewed and
   frayed state. Stand the branch *immediately* in the
   solution of glycerin and water.

The time required for processing depends on the leaves
selected but it varies from two to three days for Pear, Lilac,
and Devilwood; and three to four days for Beech and
Flowering Crabapple; to several weeks for Magnolia. The
process is an interesting one and is particularly visual in
the Pear, where the solution causes the leaves to change
dramatically from a bright green to a beautiful bronze.
When the solution has made its way through the entire
length of the spray and to the tips of the leaves, the processing has been completed. Remove the branches from the
solution, blot up the excess moisture, and bundle the stems.
Store them in a dark place, either by hanging in a closet
or laying in a box to help them retain their color.

From time to time it is necessary to add glycerin and
water in their original proportions to restore the level of the
solution and to replace the portion that has been absorbed
by the branches and leaves.

Most of the leaves that have been processed in glycerin
and water will retain their soft, supple characteristics for
years, although some tend to soften in color after long
exposure to light. For instance, the olive green of the Beech
leaves gradually becomes a lovely cinnamon brown. The
leaves are beautiful at every shade, but if your preference
is for green leaves, such as those used as a background for
the Peonies, Tulips, Delphinium, and Summer Phlox in the

arrangement in Fig. 11, plan ahead in July and August and process those extra sprays of Beech leaves that will allow you to replace the paler foliage during the winter months.

All leaves that have been processed in glycerin and water may be wiped clean with a damp cloth.

PROCESSING FOLIAGE IN SILICA GEL

WHICH FOLIAGE

Single leaves:	Hardy Cyclamen *(Cyclamen neapolitanum)*
	Ivy *(Hedera helix)*
	Maidenhair Fern *(Adiantum* spp)
	Passionflower *(Passiflora caerulea)*
	Peony *(Paeonia* spp)
Sprays of leaves:	Dusty Miller/Artemisia *(Artemisia stelleriana)*
	Rose *(Rosa* spp)
	Snow-on-the-Mountain *(Euphorbia marginata)*

HOW TO PROCESS IT

Single leaves may be wired and dried according to the directions for single flowers, p. 81; sprays of leaves, as for sprays of flowers, p. 86. Allow three days for the processing to be completed. Only the Maidenhair Fern is dried in a different way, and the technique is very simple.

MAIDENHAIR FERN
(Adiantum spp)

In most plants, silica gel removes the moisture from the flowers and foliage with which it comes in contact, generally leaving petals and leaves somewhat crisp to the touch. Leaves frequently dull a bit in drying because of the loss of the surface moisture that reflects the light from the fresh leaf and helps to give it its shiny appearance. It is interesting, then, to note that Maidenhair Fern becomes neither crisp nor dull when processed in silica gel but retains all of its soft, natural characteristics.

Drying Maidenhair Fern

Adiantum means *unwet,* and one of the curiosities of the Maidenhair Fern is that water does not adhere to its surface. This may be the factor which is responsible for the unbelievably fresh appearance of the processed Fern.

To Dry: Maidenhair Fern must be dried immediately after cutting as the tips of the fronds tend to droop readily and, once wilted, cannot be revived.

By far the easiest and most successful way I have found to process the hardy Maidenhair Fern *(Adiantum pedatum)* is in silica gel in a large fruitcake tin that will accommodate the circumference of the Fern. This requires that the container remain uncovered and so the Fern should be processed either when the humidity is low or by encasing both the Fern and container in plastic film.

Cover the bottom of the tin with a half-inch of silica gel; then hill up some more crystals slightly off center. Hold the Fern upside down. The *pedatum* part of its botanical name becomes quite evident: like a bird's foot! Note the conical, off-center fall of the fronds; rest the fronds on the crystal hill and gently spoon silica gel around and on them. When they are completely covered, rest a second Fern on top with its stem coinciding with the first. Cover as before with silica gel and add a third Fern. I have dried as many as six Ferns at one time using this method, the only limiting factor being the depth of the container. Allow two days for processing. You will be delighted with the fresh-picked, natural appearance of the Fern when the silica gel has been poured from the container.

Bind the stems with florist's tape or string, staggering the Ferns to eliminate any damage resulting from contact between the fronds; stand in oasis or hang to store.

The other kinds of Maidenhair Ferns may be processed in a tin or box that will accommodate their size and form. As with their hardier relative, multiple fronds may be processed together by layering; that is, by putting a half-inch of silica gel in the container, then a frond, another layer of silica gel, and another frond, etc. Store in a dark place until the Fern is to be used. Prolonged exposure to bright light will gradually soften the color, but the form and soft, natural appearance of the Fern will remain true for many months.

Dusty Miller/Artemisia *(Artemisia stelleriana)*	Ground Pine *(Lycopodium obscurum)*
Silver Dollar Tree/Eucalyptus *(Eucalyptus cinerea)*	Scotch Broom (Cytisus scoparius)

Although I prefer to process Artemisia in silica gel and Eucalyptus in a solution of glycerin and water, the foliage of both present an acceptable appearance when dried by hanging. Artemisia stems should be hung singly to avoid contact of the leaves with those of other stems. In contrast, six or eight sprays of Eucalyptus can be bundled together and hung to dry.

Ground Pine, one of our lovely native plants, is on the "Don't Pick" list in many states, and should be gathered only where it is legal to do so. My own supply is purchased, dried and dyed, from my florist in the late fall. The appearance of these relatively short sprays is usually flattened and stiff due to packing, but their natural grace can be restored easily by soaking them in water overnight to soften the stems which should then be shaken and their branches spread to their natural position. Depending on the desired effect, the stems can be hung or placed in oasis or styrofoam to dry.

Scotch Broom is often sought after by flower arrangers for the ease with which it can be encouraged to assume any graceful curve.

VELVET LEAVES

A foliage which I consider to be one of the most delightful for a whimsical dried bouquet is not a natural material at all but, rather, the lovely green velvet leaves such as those arranged with the Roses in Fig. 13. They are available in various sizes and shapes and should be selected to approximate most closely the natural foliage of the flower with which they are to be arranged. Velvet leaves are most accommodating; if the desired size and shape are unavailable larger sizes can be quickly and easily trimmed with a pair of scissors.

Storing Your
Dried Materials

Dried materials are more fragile than fresh ones and some care must be exercised in handling them. If you organize your dried flowers carefully when storing you will be less likely to lose your beauties through excessive handling; and if you dry flowers in any quantity, or have only very limited space, your efforts at organized storage will reap those extra cubic inches needed for "just a few more flowers."

Storage is accomplished in one of three ways and depends on the flower or plant material to be stored. It may be hung, left standing in an open container, or stored in a box. Whichever method is used it is important to cater to the form of the flower or plant material as much as possible, for the final arrangement will have far more natural beauty if careful consideration is given to form when drying and storing.

Flowers dried by bundling and hanging can be stored as they are dried until needed. It is a good idea to create a "flower filing system" to simplify your work:

STORING THE LAZY FLOWERS

1. Put materials of the same kind and color in the same bundle. This enables you to take a quick inventory of the flowers you have available for arrangements.
2. Limit the stems in each bundle to six. You can thus pick just enough flowers for a given arrangement and eliminate unnecessary handling of larger quantities of dried materials.

Winged Everlasting, Celosia, Globe Amaranth, Goldenrod, Pearly Everlasting, Statice, and Yarrow are all flowers in this category, and they hang in my attic or basement during drying and storing. See page 71.

Strawflowers, once wired, can be hung in bunches for storage. Because they flower singly and are often cut only one or a few at a time in the small garden, I find it more convenient to wire each one and stand it with others in a tall glass until they are needed. See page 71.

Wheat, Pussy Willow, and Honesty, which have stiff stems and require no processing at all, stand in vases on the closet floor, while the Reed Grass and Cattails fill the brass umbrella stand in the front hall where they present an interesting corner standing while awaiting a more permanent assignment.

STORING THE MORE EFFORT FLOWERS

Some flower dryers recommend putting the silica gel–processed flowers in tightly sealed jars to protect them from exposure to high summer humidity. There are some disadvantages to this method of storing: Pressure of the flowers against each other can cause them to become misshapen during storage. Also, many of the flowers you may wish to dry simply will not fit in jars. However, if you live in an area where the summer humidity frequently exceeds seventy percent and you have absolutely no other way to protect them, then by all means store your flowers in jars. In doing so, consideration of two small points can assure you of the greatest success:

1. Flowers stored in jars must be thoroughly dry or moisture will be trapped which can spoil all of the contents, and

2. Flowers so stored should not be wired before drying because of the potential damage to the brittle petals by the wires.

This latter is something of a disadvantage because it is infinitely easier to wire flowers when they are fresh and soft than when they are dry and brittle.

If humidity is not a serious concern then the following methods of storage are recommended:
FLOWERS "IN THE ROUND," that is, those flowers having single flowers distributed around a center stem, or that form a large flower head of cluster, such as Larkspur, Delphinium, Snapdragon, Artemisia, and Hydrangea, store best by hanging or standing individually in jars or vases. Either method of storing retains the natural distribution of the flowers on the stem and eliminates any distortion which might result from laying them in boxes, or the interference and breakage that can result from hanging two or more stems together.

Two members of the Bridal Wreath family *(Spiraea)* provide an excellent illustration of why even members of the same family sometimes require different methods of storage. The tiny flowers of Bridal Wreath, *Spiraea arguta,* appear at every angle along their woody twigs, and these should be hung individually to best retain their form. By contrast, the sprays of tiny bouquets of the later-flowering *Spiraea van houttei* have a flat underside, and their natural appearance is best catered to by laying them in a box.

I prefer to stand the stiff stems of Feverfew and Eupatorium in vases, adding the Ornamental Grasses and Queen Anne's Lace when the stems beneath the flower heads of the latter have hardened.
FLOWER HEADS THAT HAVE BEEN WIRED store best face-up in boxes, but the petals should neither lay against the bottom of the box nor press against each other. Oasis or styrofoam, purchased with the expectation of serving as the holding medium in future arrangements, can be sliced into several layers and taped to the bottom of a box to provide a temporary holder for the wire stems. Staggering the height of the flowers by bending the wire stem back along itself will enable you to put a given storage space to maximum use.

An alternate method of storing the wired flowers which eliminates both the oasis and the styrofoam is to bend the wire stem so that it becomes its own stand. Masking tape

Johnny-Jump-Ups stored in my dry garden

The wire stem of Anemone bent to form its own stand

across the wire base will anchor it firmly to the storage box. For the best adherence of the tape the box should be free of any silica gel granules. I resorted to this latter method as the number of my stored flowers increased through one growing season and my purchases of oasis and styrofoam mounted to a point where, even with the expectation of using some of these materials in later arrangements, their use as temporary holders for wired dried flowers was becoming rather expensive.

The rule that flowers must be thoroughly dry before storing is as important for flowers stored in boxes as it is for flowers stored in jars if they are to retain their fresh appearance. It is also important that dried flowers be stored when the air humidity is low so that as little moisture as possible will be trapped in the storage box. Cover the boxes with clear plastic for easy see-through identification, and label the sides as to contents. The boxes should be stored in a dry, dark place such as an inside closet. The open attic, fine for storing air-dried flowers and plant materials, is a poor place to store silica gel–processed flowers. Changes in humidity in attics are fatal to them, and one friend found only what he termed a "brown mess" when he checked his attic-stored beauties at the end of one growing season.

When storing the flowers that will be used to recreate a particular flower painting, I find it convenient to put as many of the flowers as possible in a single box, noting on its side the title of the painting or the name of the artist. This saves time later and eliminates the handling of many boxes when I am ready to create the arrangement.

The Plant It Now, Dry It Later Arrangements and How To Create Them

The pleasures derived from dried flower arrangements are greatest in the winter when the garden is dormant and fresh flowers are expensive or unavailable. I find it exciting, in November, to go into my dry garden—my Garden of Paradise where all of my dried flowers so joyously bloom together—to pick Lilies, Peonies, Statice, Roses, and so many other beauties that, when arranged, will provide us with the soft beauty of real flower decoration for many months. The question always comes to mind, "Shall I confine my arrangements to flowers of a single season or shall I ignore their fresh flowering times and take an 'anything goes' attitude, combining spring and fall, Dogwood and Chrysanthemum, in the same bouquet?" The choice is the arranger's, of course. Greenhouses long ago tampered with nature's clock, providing us with out-of-season blooms. Air freight now makes the seasons overlap and brings flowers of every clime to florists for our year-round pleasure. Certainly the possibilities of fresh flower use and design have broadened considerably.

The elegant and sophisticated Japanese flower arranging, *ikebana,* mandates that only flowers blooming in the same season may be combined in a single arrangement. Backed by a tradition of hundreds of years and with a philosophy of nature manifested in every arrangement, this exquisite Oriental art will undoubtedly continue its seasonal requirement for a very long time.

Here in the West, however, we are not quite so philosophical about our flowers, and arrangements are designed, not so much for the emotions they evoke but rather for the visual and decorative beauty they provide. I sometimes find it convenient to assume a little horticultural license and extend the blooming time of some flowers. For example, the arrangement in Fig. 13 would have been impossible to create with fresh flowers from my garden because their blooming times do not coincide: the Ranunculus were dried in late winter, the Dogwood in May, the Anemones and Shasta Daisies in June. The Baby's-Breath, Summer Phlox, Roses, and Bell Flowers were processed as they were picked throughout the summer months, and the Globe Amaranth was harvested in September. The arrangement was created in November and continued to share its colorful beauty with us until it was closeted in June in anticipation of the summer humidity.

If you prefer a conventional approach to flowers and want to retain some continuity of season in your arranging, consult the *Plant It Now, Dry It Later* calendar: "Flowers in the Order of Their Appearance in the Garden and Along the Roadside." From Pussy Willow and Daffodils in the springtime bouquet (Fig. 7) to Chrysanthemums, Japanese Bamboo, and the last Daisies of autumn (Fig. 10), the calendar will serve as a guide for your selection of flowers for seasonal arranging.

Although our minds are geared to convention and tradition, florally speaking we are standing on a threshold of a new era of design. Drying flowers opens doors to floral artistry that has never before been possible. Whether you choose to recreate a famous flower painting, the floral fashion of another era, or an arrangement of your own to complement a mélange of old and new, your dried arrangements will reflect your own joy in flowers. So experiment a little and let your imagination create something that is yours alone.

In addition to being able to pick a broad variety of

flowers from your seasonless dry garden, there are other advantages to arranging dried flowers. No longer must one be concerned with drooping flowers before the arrangement has been completed, and the artist who wishes to commit his dried arrangement to canvas no longer need share Van Gogh's frustration of painting "the whole at a flash" before the flowers fade. In fact, you may take days or weeks to complete the bouquet, and when you have tired of the design the flowers can be rearranged to something new. Another advantage is to be able to place a flower anywhere in the bouquet. A broken stem immediately relegates a fresh flower to the lower part of the arrangement if it can be used at all, but dried flower stems are as long or as short as you care to make them. See "About Stems," page 110.

Many of the flowers such as Roses, Freesias, Pansies, and Black-Eyed Susans that bloom in my dry garden will be familiar to the fresh flower arranger, but there are other colorful garden beauties such as Clematis, Hollyhock, Japanese Bamboo, and Crocus which are seldom, if ever, seen in fresh flower arranging that will add new texture and new beauty to your dried bouquet. Whether or not the *Plant It Now, Dry It Later* flowers are old favorites, they all offer opportunities to create new and exciting kinds of floral decorations that are limited only by the imagination of the arranger.

Processed foliage may be arranged in a variety of ways. For example, larger branches of Beech leaves form a background for the colorful flowers in Fig. 11; they may also be used as a filler for larger arrangements. In the recreation of Monet's *Sunflowers* (Fig. 18) single leaves or small sprays of Beech leaves were secured along the flowers' wire stems to closely approximate the natural stem foliage. Single leaves may also be arranged individually as were those of the Hardy Cyclamen in Fig. 14.

Experiment with combinations of flowers and foliage to create other interesting effects. The leaves of the Flowering Crabapple, for example, provide a particularly attractive stem foliage for pink Carnations. Many inexpensive silk flowers are available, and their texture and colors blend well with the dry flowers.

As when arranging fresh flowers, your dried flower arrangement should be suitable to its final situation and attractive at every angle from which it is viewed.

FLOWERS ARE FOR PLEASURE

There is no mysticism to arranging dried flowers, but if they are to delight the eye we should cater a bit to the tricks the eye plays in order to derive maximum visual pleasure from the completed arrangement.

Our eyes are more conscious of lines than most of us realize, and the greatest visual satisfaction will be derived from an arrangement whose stems *appear* to radiate from a focal point, much as rays of light appear to radiate from the sun. I say *appear* to radiate, for it is not necessary for the eye to *see* the point at which the stems converge, nor is it necessary for the stems to *meet* at the focal point. It is this *appearance* of radiation that gives the arrangement in the fan-shaped, five-finger container at the left so much visual appeal: the lines of the container itself guide the flower stems (and the eye) toward an imaginary focal point.

The *Plant It Now, Dry It Later* arrangements are easy to create and, in the interest of clarity, I have listed the various components—the Flowers, Foliage, Container, Mechanics, Camouflage, and Decoration, where used—with each illustrated arrangement.

Lazy Flowers arranged in a five-finger vase

CONTAINERS FOR ARRANGING

Dried arrangements can be created in any container into which you might put fresh flowers—and a vast array of others besides. Unlike fresh flower containers, those used for dried bouquets are not required to serve as a water well, and so the variety you may choose from is as broad as your imagination.

Wood, unacceptable for use with fresh flowers unless it

has a metal liner, lends its warm charm in infinite ways to the dried bouquet. Tea caddies and lovely wooden boxes of every description suddenly take on unexpected and graceful possibilities. While admiring the elegantly finished boxes, however, do not overlook the potential of wood in its simpler forms.

A favorite of mine for a small arrangement is the common pint or quart fruit box which is easily stained, painted or antiqued, depending on your taste and its final situation. The one pictured in Fig. 9 has an antique green finish and receives a dash of elegance from its blue velvet ribbon. A piece of felt cut to fit the bottom and glued into place makes these roughly finished boxes welcome anywhere.

The carefully constructed wooden planters and boxes brought home with great pride from the school woodworking class are a particular delight to fill. Most are of pine, hand-rubbed to a soft, smooth finish. If you have been reluctant to use yours for live plants because of moisture damage to the wood, fill it now with dried flowers and watch the warm glow of pleasure in the eyes of the young craftsman.

Holes drilled in driftwood gathered from the beach enable you to arrange dried flowers in unusual ways.

Baskets of many kinds are wonderful to use with dried flowers. A handsome woven duck was purchased with a metal liner but, if he were to demand fresh flowers only, I am afraid his view would be restricted to the cupboard wall. But with his back of russet Strawflowers spiked with bits of Sea Lavender and his tail of golden Yarrow his view has widened considerably, and he keeps an eye on all kitchen doings for many months of the year.

Auntie Margaret's basket of flowers under its high glass dome was always a great curiosity. The petals of each flower were sea shells set in a plasterlike substance. The shells were colored with chalks in lovely soft shades of rose, blue,

Zinnias and Black-Eyed Susans bloom in Rob's planter

The observant duck

DRIED FLOWERS UNDER GLASS

yellow, and green. Even the handle of the basket was entwined with shell Fuchsias and green fabric leaves. The heavy wire stems of these "flowers" of a century ago were held in place in the basket by shreds of that day's newspapers, and many a dreamy, romantic afternoon was spent reading the advertisements and notices of packet ships ready to take on cargo for London, Bombay, and Mauritius.

The glass domes are still with us, and arrangements of flowers under them are as interesting today as they were when Auntie Margaret was a girl growing up in India. I used one of these domes to capture a sentimental moment for a friend who had kept the top of her wedding cake carefully stored away for years in the hope of "doing something with it someday." We recreated her wedding bouquet of white Freesia, white Roses, and blue Bachelor's Buttons, and arranged it with the bride and groom under glass, to this friend's unending delight.

If you want to cover an arrangement with glass, but the Victorian dome is not to your liking, try the covered cheese and butter dishes, Fig. 12, but avoid those which are cut or etched. Other interesting shapes in covered glass are the apples, pears, and eggs. (Fig. 15.) Tightly sealed, they will keep dust and humidity from your dried flowers.

One of the most practical and versatile containers for a circular arrangement is an inexpensive glass bowl (about 4″ in diameter) or of a size to fit into your more elegant centerpiece containers. An arrangement created in such a bowl takes on a new personality as it moves from crystal to silver to the round gravy boat or to some other serving piece which matches your dinnerware.

Among my favorite flower containers for traditional arrangements are the charming pottery pieces of eighteenth-century design so often associated with Colonial Williamsburg, the five-finger vases, and the Delft flower bricks and jardinieres.

Teacups are delightful containers for small arrangements. Fruit dishes, normally too shallow for fresh flower

Other containers for arranging

arranging, take on a new life when filled with dried materials. (Fig. 13.)

Keep a sharp eye out for the attractive bottles used today to package all kinds of beverages. Colored and milk glass, and brown crocks, such as the Portuguese wine crock in Fig. 10, can be very welcome additions to your flower container collection. Red clay flower pots are also fun to use; they are inexpensive and readily available.

"One man's trash is another man's treasure" was never truer than when applied to flower containers. Rummage sales and thrift shops are often sources for particularly interesting and inexpensive flower holders. A single champagne glass, the sole survivor of years of partying, has little value to the hostess, but it can take a new lease on life as a flower holder.

The warmth of old copper, brass, and pewter makes containers of these metals highly acceptable for dried arrangements. The pierced brass boxes from India, copper ewers from Lebanon and Greece, pewter mugs from England, and that ancient, leaky copper kettle from the country are among the unexpected items that can be used.

Each of us has a preference, and mine runs to the French tole cachepots and flower containers. Many fine reproductions of the originals are available and they are a particular delight for me to fill.

Copper ewer features an arrangement of Sunflowers

Tins of various sizes, tastefully covered with wallpaper (the Contact types are especially easy to use) or fabric, perhaps to match a room, and touched with a bit of velvet ribbon around the top and bottom edges, can provide a decorator touch wherever it is placed. Use small, rather than large, prints for the best effect. Let your imagination go a little in designing your container. Without water as a necessary consideration, include the papier mâché and pasteboard boxes in your thinking. They are available in many sizes but I especially like the round ones that look like small hatboxes. Ingenuity and originality kept in good taste can give as much satisfaction to the flower container designer as the dried flowers themselves.

Flower arrangers always have an eye out for containers as they travel, and arrangements created in these containers —which are sometimes toted home at considerable effort— give a double pleasure. Not only are the flowers enjoyed but the container brings back memories of happy and exciting events. Your dried flowers will give these treasures wider usefulness and greater continuous enjoyment.

MECHANICS

The mechanics are (1) the holding mediums that serve to hold the stems of the dried materials in the *Plant It Now, Dry It Later* arrangements, and (2) any other devices needed to anchor the arrangement to its container.

The holding mediums most useful to the dried flower arranger are styrofoam, oasis, sand, and Posey Klay. The kenzan, or Japanese needlepoint holder, is widely used in fresh flower arranging, where the soft flower stems are easily impaled on its needlelike points; it is also used in dried flower arranging but in a quite different way. The stems of dried materials are hard, brittle, and often made of wire, and so the kenzan has little direct value as a stem holder. However, when it is set firmly in place in the container on a bit of Posey Klay, the lead-weighted kenzan becomes a holder for the styrofoam or oasis and an anchor for a top-heavy or asymmetrical arrangement which might otherwise tilt or slip from place. The final choice of the holding medium to be used, and whether or not a kenzan is needed, is determined largely by the shape of the container.

OPEN-MOUTHED CONTAINERS

I prefer to use oasis and styrofoam as the holding medium for open-mouthed containers such as the milk glass compote in Fig. 13. Both are lightweight, porous, and easily cut with a kitchen knife. They should be set securely in place before the arrangement is begun.

Oasis is easier to use than styrofoam in containers such

as baskets, wooden boxes, and flower pots because it compresses slightly. When cut just a bit larger than the container it can be wedged tightly in place, thereby eliminating the need for further anchoring.

When using shallow bowls, urns, or irregularly shaped containers, it is virtually impossible to have a snug fit between the holding medium and the container, and so the styrofoam or oasis must be anchored in place either by the use of the kenzan as described above or by crisscrossing transparent tape across the holding medium and extending it an inch or two down the outside of the container. A brick of styrofoam anchored to the bottom of a brass urn by my heaviest kenzan set on a bit of Posey Klay holds erect a top-heavy arrangement of Reed Grass and Bittersweet.

Sand is the best holding medium for stems when the arrangement is created in a closed-mouth container such as a five-finger vase, the narrow-necked crock in Fig. 10, or a Williamsburg flower brick whose holes do not provide sufficient support to hold the stems in place. Sand is preferred, too, for the arrangement in a clear glass bowl, where other mechanics, unless camouflaged, would detract from its appearance. In a pinch, of course, sugar, table salt, or another granular substance will serve as an able substitute for sand.

CLOSE-MOUTHED CONTAINERS

The mechanics are very much in evidence when the arrangement is created in a covered glass container such as that in Fig. 12, or on a wooden surface. The most satisfactory and least conspicuous material to use here is Posey Klay which, when pressed to the surface, performs a double function: (1) as a holding medium for the stems, and (2) as an anchor for the arrangement. The Posey Klay remains soft after long exposure to air and has the advantage of not

GLASS CONTAINERS AND WOOD SURFACES

staining any metal, wood, or glass surface with which it comes in contact.

CAMOUFLAGING THE MECHANICS

The mechanics should not be in evidence when the arrangement has been completed. Happily, it is easier to hide them when arranging dried flowers than it is when arranging fresh flowers. Moss, dried in sheets and dyed, and available from the florist, is my favorite camouflage for covering the mechanics used in arranging flowers in open containers as in Figs. 7 and 15. Moss is not the only possibility, however, and sand was used to camouflage the mechanics in the arrangement of Queen Anne's Lace in Fig. 8. The choice here was dictated by the fact that Queen Anne's Lace is found growing in dry, sunny, sandy places, and the use of sand presented a far more natural setting for these flowers than Moss, which has overtones of lushness and shade.

Sometimes the massing of flower heads in an arrangement (as in Fig. 11) hides the mechanics, thereby eliminating the need for additional camouflage and making its use optional.

The holding medium used in closed-mouth containers such as the five-finger vase on page 104 and the wine crock in Fig. 10 is usually sand, but whatever holding medium is selected it remains unseen by virtue of the shape and opaqueness of the container. In the event that a clear glass, closed-mouth container is selected for an arrangement, fill it almost to the top with sand which, because it is a natural material, is acceptable both as a holding medium and as a camouflage.

ABOUT STEMS

One of the delights of dried flower arranging is the freedom to put a flower virtually anywhere in the bouquet. Short-stemmed flowers can turn up in tall places, raising a momentary question in the mind of even the most experienced gardener: "How did you ever grow such *tall* Rock Cress?"

Obviously the snips take care of the stems that are too long for proper placement of the flower in the arrangement, but what of the stems that are too short?

Unless the arrangement is to be a low cluster of flower heads such as that in Fig. 13, it is probable that the wire stem which replaced the natural stem of the flower dried in silica gel will be too short. Also, long sprays of Delphinium, cut just below the bottom flower to save on the quantity of silica gel needed for processing, require additional stem length to enable the arranger to place them properly in the bouquet.

There are several methods of lengthening stems. The choice depends in part on the stem, and whether or not it will be visible when the arrangement has been completed. Whenever possible, select the method that will enable the flower to present the most natural appearance in the bouquet.

WIRE STEMS

The flexibility of wire permits the flower to assume any angle or attitude the arranger desires, and so it is the preferred method of lengthening the stems of most of the flowers that have been processed in silica gel.

Cut a length of #23 wire as long as the desired stem. If the stem is to be longer than six to seven inches it is wise to use a double thickness or a heavier wire if it is available. This wire is then bound the full length of the flower's short wire stem with florist's tape in the following manner:

(1) Hold the short wire stem and the wire together between the thumb and forefinger of the left hand, at the point where the short wire enters the natural stem of the flower.

(2) Place the end of the florist's tape under the left thumb so that it covers the juncture of the natural and wire stems, and begin rotating the wire in a clockwise direction, stretching the tape slightly while pulling downward with the right hand to wind the tape along the length of the wires. Use

Lengthening a wire stem

either green or brown florist's tape, whichever best duplicates the flower's natural stem.

Wire stems that will not show in the final arrangement need not be wrapped for the entire length of the added wire stem. Wrap them only as far as is necessary to bind the short wire stem and its extension together.

NATURAL STEMS

A number of flowers and other plant materials have hollow stems which can be used as holders to extend the length of the stems of either the Lazy or More Effort Flowers.

When processing Anemone, Marigolds, and Zinnia, I remove the foliage from the stems and set them aside to dry. The hollow stems of these plants will stiffen, harden, and shrink a bit, but they are excellent wire stem holders while at the same time providing a natural appearance in the bouquet.

The stiff, tubular stems of Wheat and Reed Grass do not shrink, and may be used for arranging immediately after they have been cut. Wheat can be used as a holder for either wire-stemmed, hollow, or solid-stemmed materials, and in the case of the Delphinium instant length can be added by slipping the Wheat well up into the thick, hollow Delphinium stalk.

I use the bamboolike stems of the Reed Grass as a holder for the solid, sturdy, but often too-short stems of the Bittersweet when I want to place the bright berries somewhere other than at the bottom of an arrangement.

Dogwood blossoms can be reattached to Dogwood branches—use brown florist's tape to match the branch—and stiff twigs and branches of trees can always be substituted for wire stems if desired.

PREFABRICATE SPRAYS WHERE POSSIBLE

It is wise to prefabricate sprays of dried flowers whenever possible before placing them in an arrangement. This is particularly true for the wire-stemmed More Effort Flowers.

In effect, prefabrication substitutes a single stem for several stems and eliminates much of the "put-it-in, pull-it-out, put-it-in-again" kind of overhandling that flowers sometimes undergo when they are arranged individually, and which can be so shattering to the more brittle dried flower petals.

To prefabricate a spray of flowers simply
1. decide what the relative position of the flowers in the spray should be, and
2. bind their wire stems together with florist's tape as described in "About Stems," above, adding additional wire, if necessary, to achieve the required stem length.

If the position of a flower in the spray is not quite satisfactory when the arrangement has been completed it is still possible to make an adjustment without removing the spray. Simply bend the flower's wire stem until the desired position is achieved. If fingers are too large to fit into small places use a pair of tweezers to bend the wire stem.

Examples of prefabricated sprays of More Effort Flowers that appear in the *Plant It Now, Dry It Later* arrangements are the Shasta Daisies and Chrysanthemums in Fig. 10 and the Peonies and Roses in Fig. 11.

Dried flowers also offer an opportunity for unusual regroupings that might prompt even nature to take a second glance. For example, I enjoy the color and form of the Bell Flower *(Platycodon grandiflorum)* and often use it in interesting ways in the dried bouquet. When fresh, the use of the flower is somewhat limited by its spiky habit of growth. When dry, however, I am able to regroup the flowers into small sprays or clusters, which broadens their use considerably.

While the prefabrication of stems usually applies to the wire stems of the More Effort Flowers, there are times when it is useful to prefabricate the natural stems of Lazy Flowers (or the wire stems of Strawflowers).

For example, the tiny white flower of Winged Everlasting is almost lost when placed in an arrangement alone, and adding the many single stems of this flower that are necessary to form a cluster is not only time consuming when creating an arrangement but it also contributes to the dangers of overhandling mentioned above. You will find it far easier to form a flower cluster of the desired size, binding the stems together to create a single stem before placing it in the arrangement.

REPAIRS AND REINFORCEMENTS

The final appearance of any floral arrangement, whether the materials are fresh or dried, depends to a large degree on the condition and appearance of the materials of which it is composed. It goes without saying that the loose petal, the frayed or perforated leaf, or the Delphinium stalk whose tip has broken at the last moment will detract from the overall attractive appearance of an arrangement. In the case of dried materials, many of these problems can be solved in unbelievably simple ways, and so, unless it is a matter of a completely shattered flower, the arranger can usually salvage his dried flower materials by making modest repairs, whereas their fresh counterparts might well have to be discarded.

REPAIRS

LOOSE PETALS

If careful attention is given to "Timing," page 79, and to "Spilling the silica gel" (page 87) from the flowers when the processing has been completed, there should be little need to glue loose or fallen petals back in place. Upon occasion I will stretch the timing a bit and pick a Rose when it is almost full blown, knowing only too well that in doing so I should expect to find that a petal or two have loosened during the processing. But the small effort necessary to apply a dot or two of Elmer's Glue-All or melted paraffin to a loose petal to reestablish its position is more than rewarded by the beauty of the almost full-blown Rose. Roses, of course, are not the only flowers that can lose a petal, and the use of Elmer's Glue or melted paraffin can be applied to all.

FRAYED OR TATTERED LEAVES AND PETALS

The torn or frayed edges of leaves that have been processed in glycerin and water are easily trimmed with scissors but every effort should be made to retain the *shape* of the leaf even if its *size* is sharply reduced by the cutting.

The appearance of fragmented petal edges can be improved by careful trimming, again giving careful attention to retaining the petal shape.

BROKEN DELPHINIUM TIPS

A careless motion can quickly part a Delphinium tip from the rest of the stalk, thereby presenting what appears to be an insoluble problem. But not so! As noted in "About Stems" the Delphinium stalk is hollow. Near its tip the stalk diameter is very small. Cut a two-inch length of wire; slip one end into the broken tip and the other end into the stalk. The two broken ends of the stalk should meet and resume an unbroken appearance. If they do not meet shorten the wire by an appropriate amount to effect the reconciliation.

REINFORCEMENTS

There are a few plant materials which, because of the shrinkage of some of their parts during the drying process, require some reinforcement to help them present their best appearance in the arrangement or to increase the ease with which they may be handled.

CORN

When the ear is left on the stalk for drying and subsequent arranging, it must be secured to the inch or two of stalk remaining above the ear if the droopy appearance it would otherwise present after drying is to be avoided. After the husk has been drawn back from the ear, and the silk removed, secure the ear to the short remaining stalk with fine wire before hanging to dry.

FRAGILE STEMS

"An ounce of prevention is worth a pound of cure," and this old adage can be applied to the treatment of the fragile stems of some dried flowers, such as those of the Crocus, whose moisture-heavy stems undergo considerable shrinkage during the drying process. Later shattering of these stems when handling and arranging can be eliminated if melted paraffin is applied along the stem with a cotton Q-tip before the flower is stored.

Additional reinforcement of petals with respect to petals, or petals with respect to stem, can be achieved with a bit of melted paraffin applied to the underside of the outer petals, as described under "Tulip," page 149.

DECORATIONS

Plant It Now, Dry It Later decorations are the supplemental, floral or non-floral materials, other than the container, which may be used to enhance the final appearance of an arrangement.

The decorations can take many forms. They are the butterflies in the Flemish-style arrangement in Fig. 11, and the velvet ribbon that graces the pint box in Fig. 9. They include the quartz seen with the Queen Anne's Lace in Fig. 8, and the teakwood base upon which the Oriental-style arrangement in Fig. 10 stands.

The use of the base or pedestal in Japanese flower arranging had its origin in the Shinto and Buddhist religions where it was a mark of respect to set one's floral offering on a pedestal before a shrine. Bases or pedestals take many forms, from a polished or lacquered slab of wood to the more elaborately carved wooden stands. Tiles, marble, and other flat-surfaced materials can also be used as bases. Curiously, baskets were excused from this customary use of the base in Japanese flower arranging by the decision of an early Japanese emperor who, as the story goes, was so enchanted with his newly arrived baskets from China that he issued an edict permitting them to stand without pedestals! Whether it is fact or fiction, the story is an indication of the important role which flower arranging has played in the culture of Japan over the centuries.

Once processed, most of the Lazy and More Effort Flowers undergo little change in color when exposed to normal daylight and soften ever so slightly when the exposure is for prolonged periods of time. There are some exceptions, of course, as with the Goldenrod losing much of its mustard-yellow hue, but the change is so gradual that it is virtually imperceptible. A contrasting color surprise is the blues. Often a difficult dye color for fabrics and paints because of its tendency to fade, the natural blues of the flowers are among the strongest of colors and show almost no inclination toward fading. However, the colors of the *Plant It Now, Dry It Later* flowers are affected by direct sunlight, and the flowers should never be exposed to the rays of the sun for any length of time.

FADING

Exposure to high summer humidity (above seventy percent) over prolonged periods has little effect on the color of the Lazy Flowers, but it does tend to "wash out" some of the colors of the More Effort Flowers as well as to spoil their form. Arrangements of More Effort Flowers (except those in sealed glass containers) must be carefully stored and protected during the summer in those areas where the humidity is high if they are to be expected to present an attractive appearance the following winter.

The Plant It Now, Dry It Later Arrangements

A re-creation of Jan Brueghel's painting *Flowers in a Blue Vase*.

Twentieth-century flowers arranged in the manner
of the seventeenth-century Flemish flower painters.

Joi's first corsage, a delightful memento of a happy event.

Shasta Daisies, Chrysanthemums, and Japanese Bamboo, all PLANT IT NOW, DRY IT LATER flowers, arranged in an oriental manner.

Orange and yellow Marigolds and magenta Globe Amaranth arranged in a simple wooden pint box.

An adaptation of Robert Furber's *Twelve Months of Flowers*. PLANT IT
NOW, DRY IT LATER flowers selected from all twelve months of Furber's
catalogue are arranged in a spectrum of floral seasons: from the spring-
flowering Dog's Tooth Violet, Anemone, Narcissus, and Crocus on the
left, to the late-summer and autumn-flowering Marigold, Bachelor's Button,
Cockscomb, and Goldenrod on the right.

The fashionable flowers recommended to London gardeners for June blooming in 1730. The arrangement is one of a series of monthly illustrations from Robert Furber's nursery catalogue *Twelve Months of Flowers*.

A compote of garden flowers.

Spring-flowering and autumn-flowering Crocus bloom together amidst sprays of Acacia in a glass apple.

My Sunflowers! A re-creation of Claude Monet's painting *Sunflowers*.

A Viking ship with sheets of Pussy Willow under full sail, her Daffodil
passengers bent against the wind.

Charming arrangements of LAZY flowers:
A sunny bouquet in a tiny watering can features yellow Acroclinium, Immortelle, and Statice
spiked with royal blue Starflowers and white Baby's Breath. A corsage of orange-toned
Strawflowers, yellow Immortelle and Statice, with Starflowers in natural and orange tones,
in an "antique" French jewel box. A basket of ever-blooming purple and yellow Statice,
magenta and pink Globe Amaranth, pink and white Rhodanthe, yellow Acroclinium, white
Baby's Breath and Sea Lavender.

Sunflowers, Reed Grass, Wheat, Corn, Eucalyptus, and Peacock feathers arranged in a floor-standing copper ewer. The Sunflower in the background is from the herbal *Hortus Eystettensis*, printed in Eichstatt, Germany, in 1613. The poster-size reproduction is one of a series of botanical prints published by the New York Botanical Garden.

A Viking Ship with Sheets of Pussywillow
under Full Sail, Her Daffodil Passengers
Bent against the Wind.

A Pussywillow branch will assume almost any desired curve if a fine wire is strung between the two ends of a fresh-cut branch and the branch is hung or set aside until it has dried. Drying takes two to three weeks.

Figure 7

FLOWERS: From your own garden or the local florist:
3 sprays of Pussywillow
5 Daffodils
CONTAINER: A Viking ship

MECHANICS: Posey Klay, kenzan, Oasis (or Styrofoam)
CAMOUFLAGE: Moss
DECORATION: Mirror pedestal

STEP I Center the Posey Klay, kenzan, and Oasis in the container

STEP II Cover the mechanics with Moss
STEP III Arrange Pussywillow and Daffodils

An Arrangement of a *Plant It Now, Dry It Later* Wildflower: Queen Anne's Lace.

It is evident from this arrangement of Queen Anne's Lace, gathered from along the roadside, that it is not necessary to have a garden at all to enjoy the decorative beauty of dried flowers.

FLOWERS: From everyone's roadside garden:
24 Queen Anne's Lace, dried in varying stages of development
CONTAINER: A low, open dish

MECHANICS: Posey Klay, kenzan, Oasis or Styrofoam)
CAMOUFLAGE: Sand
DECORATION: Quartz mineral

Figure 8

Oasis (or Styrofoam), held firmly in place in the container by a kenzan and Posey Klay, is the holding medium for the stiff flower stems. Place these mechanics off-center in the container, as shown, to increase the visual interest of the arrangement.

Sand serves to camouflage the mechanics and to add a touch of realism to this arrangement of familiar roadside beauties.

Box of Marigolds and Globe Amaranth.

FLOWERS: From your own garden:
4 yellow Marigolds
7 orange Marigolds
Magenta Globe Amaranth
CONTAINER: Common wood pint box, antiqued olive green

MECHANICS: Oasis
CAMOUFLAGE: Moss
DECORATION: 1 yard blue velvet ribbon; 1 square of felt cut slightly smaller than the bottom of the box

STEP I Glue the felt to the bottom of the box to smooth an otherwise rough surface.
STEP II Cut the Oasis slightly larger than the box and press it firmly in place.
STEP III Tie the velvet ribbon around the upper rim of the box. Touch the underside of the ribbon with a dab of glue to prevent it from sliding.
STEP IV Cover the Oasis with Moss and tuck bits of Moss into the four corners of the box.
STEP V Arrange the Marigolds, then add the stems of the Globe Amaranth.

Figure 9

Plant It Now, Dry It Later Flowers Arranged in the Oriental Manner.

A bit of global sleight-of-hand created this Japanese-style arrangement whose uncluttered appearance allows the beauty of each floral material to be fully enjoyed.

FLOWERS: From your own garden:
5 sprays, Japanese Bamboo
3 yellow Chrysanthemums
3 Shasta Daisies
CONTAINER: Portuguese wine crock

MECHANICS: Sand
DECORATION: Chinese carved teakwood base

STEP I Fill container to its neck with sand.
STEP II Arrange the sprays of Japanese Bamboo.
STEP III Wrap each wire stem with florists tape and prefabricate the sprays of Chrysanthemums and Shasta Daisies. Arrange. Adjustments in the relative positions of the Chrysanthemums and Shasta Daisies can be made by bending their wire stems after the arrangement has been completed. See "Prefabricate Sprays Where Possible."
STEP IV Stand the completed arrangement upon its base.

Figure 10

Twentieth-Century *Plant It Now, Dry It Later Flowers* Arranged in the Manner of the Seventeenth-Century Flemish Flower Painters.

Flemish artists painted their flowers from many angles in an effort to reveal the flower's structure as well as to portray its beauty. This same effect is easily achieved in dried flower arranging simply by bending the wire stems of the flowers to the desired angle. Note the profiles of the Tulips and Peony.

Figure 11

Always to be found in the Flemish flower paintings is a butterfly or two, a ladybug, or some other small creature which lend a bit of realism to the painting. Three butterflies are seen in this adaptation of Flemish floral artistry.* Whenever I can find them in the lawn or in the garden, I substitute the buglike pupal shells shed by the locusts during the summer for the butterflies, for these latter beauties, like our wildflowers, are decreasing in population wherever man expands his trappings of civilization.

Another realistic touch to these paintings is found in the bits of floral odds and ends that appear to have fallen from place in the arrangement—or perhaps they were carelessly left behind by the arranger?—the unused flower, the detached petal, or the torn leaf.

FLOWERS: From your own garden:
5 sprays Delphinium
2 rose-colored Tree Peonies
1 shell-pink herbaceous Peony
2 white herbaceous Peonies
3 Tulips, white edged in pink
3 purple Anemones
2 pink Roses
Sprays of Summer Phlox
FOLIAGE: Beech leaves
Eucalyptus
CONTAINER: Ceramic vase
MECHANICS: Posey Klay, kenzan, and Oasis or Styrofoam
DECORATION: Butterflies, floral odds and ends

---

*Butterflies pictured are:
  Monarch *(Danaus plexippus)*
  Eastern Swallowtail *(Papilio polyxenes asterius)*
  Sulphur *(Colias philodice)*

STEP I Secure the mechanics in the container.

STEP II Create the outline of the arrangement with the stalks of Delphinium, Beech leaves, and Eucalyptus.

STEP III Prefabricate separately, and arrange, the sprays of Tree Peonies, the rose-colored herbaceous Peonies, and the Roses.

STEP IV Add the remaining Peonies, the Tulips, Anemones, and Summer Phlox.

STEP V Glue the butterflies in place.

Joi's First Corsage

Figure 12

Joi felt her first corsage was "the most lovely thing" she had ever seen. With ribbon removed, the corsage was processed in silica gel for five days, then left standing in air for another week to allow all parts to harden. A thin coating of melted paraffin was applied to the leaves to restore their sheen. A drop of Elmer's Glue-All fastened the corsage securely to the lavender painted base of a covered cheese dish. The rim of the glass cover was coated with Touch-n-Glue to assure a tight bond between cover and base, thereby protecting the corsage from dampness and dust. Moss green and lavender velvet ribbon add a bit of elegance.

Hardy Cyclamen Flowers and Leaves with a Wisp of Sea Lavender

FLOWERS: From your own garden:
3 Hardy Cyclamen
1 Spray Sea Lavender
FOLIAGE: 3 Hardy Cyclamen leaves

CONTAINER: Teakwood pedestal
MECHANICS: Posey Klay
DECORATION: Japanese washed stones; Oriental ceramic figurine

STEP I Press the Posey Klay to the pedestal base.

STEP II Arrange flowers and leaves.

STEP III Glue stones in place.

Figure 14

Figure 13

A Compote of Garden Flowers

FLOWERS: From your own garden:
1. Bell Flower
2. Rose
3. Summer Phlox
4. Ranunculus
5. Anemone
6. Globe Amaranth
7. Shasta Daisy
8. Dogwood
9. Baby's-Breath used as a filler
FOLIAGE: Velvet leaves
CONTAINER: Milk Glass Compote
MECHANICS: Oasis or Styrofoam

STEP I Secure Oasis to container by crisscrossing with transparent tape.

STEP II Prefabricate Roses and velvet leaves.
STEP III: Arrange the flowers.

Arrangements
Under Glass

It is not necessary to dry the *Plant It Now, Dry It Later* flowers on a grand scale to enjoy their year-round beauty. Most of the glass containers I use—the eggs, apples, and pears—accommodate only mini-arrangements, but the pleasure to be derived from these gemlike treasures is often as great as that which one receives from the larger arrangements. You will be surprised at the dimension that small drying efforts and left-over materials can have when arranged in these attractive glass containers. The single Delphinium flower, processed alone or left over from a larger arrangement, suddenly becomes important. Bits of other floral materials, such as small sprays of Acacia and Sea Lavender, too small for use elsewhere, take on a new significance. Note the Acacia which serves as a filler for the arrangement of Crocus in Fig. 15.

If you live in an area where summer humidity is high, arranging the Crocus, Azalea, Lenten Rose, and other spring flowers under glass when the heat is still on, and sealing the container, will enable you to preserve these More Effort Flowers for year-round enjoyment.

HOW TO CREATE ARRANGEMENTS IN EGGS, APPLES & PEARS

Be certain that all flowers are thoroughly dry before arranging them. The arrangements should be done when the humidity is low so that as little moisture as possible will be introduced into the container. I create these arrangements when the heat is on, either in the spring using spring flowers—the Dog's-Tooth Violet, Pansy, Rock Cress and May Apple—or late in the fall after the last flowers have been harvested.

Flowers under glass are almost always arranged "in the round," that is, they should be attractive when viewed from any angle. The arrangement should be created before it is placed in the container.

Arrangements in glass are exquisite for your own pleasure, as gifts for friends, or for religious and charitable bazaars. They are easy to arrange and easy to store until you are ready to give them.

Creating the arrangement

Press a piece of Posey Klay about the diameter of a silver dollar, a half-inch thick in the center and tapered along the edge, on a piece of paper. Tear a bit of Moss large enough to cover the Posey Klay and with a dab of Elmer's Glue-All secure the moss to the Posey Klay. Press the pointed end of a pencil (or an artist's brush as was used at left) into the approximate center of this base. This will serve later as a handle to lower the arrangement into the container.

Bits of Acacia, Sea Lavender, or other filler material, kept low, will give a feeling of weight to the arrangement. If you do not use a filler material be sure that some flowers are placed close to the moss to avoid a top-heavy appearance.

Placing it in the container

When the arrangement has been completed put a spot or two of Elmer's Glue in the bottom of the container, lift the arrangement by its handle, peel the paper from the bottom of the Posey Klay, and lower it into the container. When you are satisfied that the arrangement is properly centered and angled, allow the glue to dry and then carefully twist and remove the pencil.

Spring-Flowering and Autumn-Flowering
Crocus Bloom Together in This *Plant It
Now, Dry It Later* Arrangement under
Glass.

FLOWERS: From your own garden:
  3 white Spring-Flowering Crocus
  3 lavender Autumn-Flowering
  Crocus
  Small sprays of Acacia

CONTAINER: Glass apple
MECHANICS: Posey Klay
CAMOUFLAGE: Moss
DECORATION: Bird

Figure 15

Recreating Famous Flower Paintings and Floral Fashions of Other Eras

The recreation of famous flower paintings and the floral fashions of other eras is the epitome of the flower dryer's art. I hasten to add, however, that this last phrase does not imply that extraordinary artistic, gardening, or flower drying talents are necessary to recreate flower paintings. The results of this kind of dried flower arranging often prove most satisfying, particularly to the novice, because the artistic talent in arranging the flowers has already been provided by the artist whose arrangement you have selected to recreate; gardening talent is not a necessary prerequisite, for it is possible to recreate some famous flower paintings without ever turning a garden fork! For example, the Sunflower in Claude Monet's painting on page 29 grows in many parts of the United States in everyone's roadside garden; and the Anemones and Daisies so popular with Raoul Dufy and other modern artists are available from the local florist. In contrast, virtually all of the flowers in Furber's eighteenth-century bouquets and in Brueghel's *Flowers in a Blue Vase* are popular flowers to grow in your own garden.

It is easy to see, then, that the successful recreation of famous flower paintings is primarily a matter of (1) identifying the flowers in the painting and knowing which of these will dry well, and (2) knowing the techniques of drying and arranging them. But how many of us, while admiring Jan Brueghel's *Flowers in a Blue Vase,* can readily identify the rare and common flowers of the seventeenth century that he painted? Brueghel emphasized the many and varied forms of Narcissus, Tulip, and Iris in *Flowers in a Blue Vase*. Listed below are the *kinds* of flowers which appear in the recreation of this famous painting.

Figure 16

A RECREATION OF JAN BRUEGHEL'S
Flowers in a Blue Vase

Silk Iris complement the *Plant It Now, Dry It Later* flowers gathered from my dry garden. The blue vase, although new, is the same kind of Greek pottery as the one in which Brueghel arranged his flowers. Its design, in bas relief, represents the wars between the Greeks and the Trojans.

Key to Figure 16
1. Johnny-Jump-Up *(Viola tricolor* var *hortensis)*
2. Alkanet *(Anchusa officinalis)*
3. Scilla *(Scilla sibirica)*

4. Narcissus *(Narcissus poeticus)*
5. Narcissus *(Narcissus triandrus)*
6. Rock Cress *(Arabis alpina)*
7. Ranunculus *(Ranunculus)*
8. Checker Lily *(Fritillaria meleagris)*
9. Narcissus *(Narcissus triandrus)*, Angel's Tears
10. Iris
11. Tulip, Lily-flowered *(Tulipa acuminata)*
12. Summer Snowflake *(Leucojum aestivum)*
13. Anemone *(Anemone)*
14. Tulip *(Tulipa)*
15. Spring Phlox *(Phlox divaricata)*
16. Rose foliage *(Rosa)*
17. Sweet Rocket *(Hesperis matronalis)*
Butterflies:
18. Gulf Fritillary *(Agraulis vanillae)*
19. American Painted Lady *(Vanessa cardui)*

Robert Furber's *Twelve Months of Flowers*

Furber's catalogue illustrates the kinds of flowers that were popular in England's gardens in the early eighteenth century, and identifies them by names commonly in vogue when the catalogue was published in 1730. Many of his offerings are favorites that grace our gardens today. Although the species and/or varieties of flowers may be different from those I have dried—and this is particularly true of the Tulip and the Rose—the *kinds* are the same. Dry your own favorites of these same kinds of flowers to recreate the floral fashion of Furber's England.

"June" from Robert Furber's
Twelve Months of Flowers

Furber's Common Names	*Today's Common Names*
The Lesser black Hellebore	Christmas Rose
Acacia or sweet button tree	Acacia
Double Stock	Double Stock
Duke Vantol Tulip	Lily-Flowered Tulip, red and yellow
White Crocus	Spring-Flowering Crocus, white
Single Anemone	Single Anemone, purple and white
Yellow dutch Crocus	Crocus, yellow
White Dens Caninus	Dog's-Tooth Violet, white
Single Prusian blew Anemone	Single Anemone, blue

Double Narcissus of Constantinople	Poet Narcissus, double white
White Boslamon Narciss	Poet Narcissus, white with yellow trumpet
Rhyven Narciss	Poet Narcissus, yellow
Goldfinch Polyanthos	Primrose, peachy-yellow
Best Claremon Tulip	Tulip, red with white markings
The Checker'd Fritillaria	Checker Lily
Palto Auri flame Tulip	Tulip, yellow and red
Single Orange Narcissus	Single Poet Narcissus, orange
Single Junquill	Poet Narcissus, yellow with orange cup
Double Junquill	Double Narcissus, yellow
Columbine Strip'd	Columbine, common lavender
Dutch yellow Ranunculus	Ranunculus, large double yellow
Mountain bulbed Crow foot	Ranunculus, yellow
Indian Queen Ranunculus	Ranunculus, large double pink
Indian King Ranunculus	Ranunculus, large double pink
Red Austrian rose	Rose, single red
Yellow globe flower	Globeflower
Dwarf Dutch Tulip	Dwarf Tulip
Blew-bell Hyacinth	Scilla, blue
Scarlet Geranium	Geranium, red
Blew Corn flower	Bachelor's Button, blue
Double blew Larkspur	Larkspur, blue
White Batchelors Button	Bachelor's Button, white
Purple Coxcomb Amaranth	Cockscomb, purplish-red
Double fether few	Feverfew, double
Three leav'd Passion flower	Passionflower
Hearts ease	Johnny-Jump-Up
Yellow Amaranthus	Cockscomb, yellow
White monthly Rose	Rose, white
Hardy golden Rod	Goldenrod
Quill'd African Marigold	Marigold, yellow
White Eternal	Pearly Everlasting
Purple Amaranthoides	Globe Amaranth, magenta
African Marigold	Marigold, yellow
Michaelmas Daisie	Michaelmas Daisy, blue
Spiked Aster	New England Aster, blue
Holly hock always double	Hollyhock, double rose
Musk scabiosus	Scabiosa, lavender
Saffron flower	Autumn-Flowering Crocus, blue
Scarlet single Anemone	Single Anemone, red
Single blew Anemone	Single Anemone, blue

Scarlet Althaea
Perennial dwarf Sun flower
Great Purple Crane's Bill
Yellow round Eternal
Single purple Anemone
Monthly rose bud

Rose of Sharon, rosy-red
Black-Eyed Susan
Wild Geranium, purple
Immortelle
Small single Anemone, purple
Rosebud

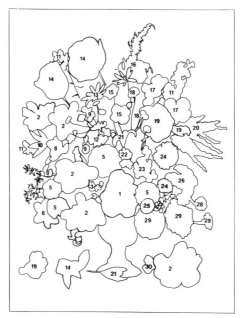

Figure 17

An Adaptation of Furber's *Twelve Months of Flowers*

The choice of fresh flowers available for arranging in the early eighteenth century depended upon the season. A dry garden is seasonless, however, and this adaptation of Furber's *Twelve Months of Flowers* spans the entire year.

Key to Figure 17:
1. Rose
2. Anemone
3. Johnny-Jump-Up
4. Dog's-Tooth Violet
5. Ranunculus
6. Narcissus
7. Scilla
8. Crocus, Spring-Flowering
9. Feverfew, double
10. Tulip, dwarf
11. Larkspur
12. Cowslip
13. Black-Eyed Susan
14. Tulip
15. Globeflower
16. Celosia, Plumed
17. New England Aster
18. Globe Amaranth
19. Rose of Sharon
20. Goldenrod
21. Crocus, Autumn-Flowering
22. Pearly Everlasting
23. Immortelle
24. Calendula
25. Pincushion Flower
26. Cockscomb
27. Summer Phlox
28. Bachelor's Button
29. Marigold
30. Rose foliage

Claude Monet's *Sunflowers*—and Mine

Figure 18. *My* Sunflowers!

In 1881 the French Impressionist Claude Monet painted his famous *Sunflowers.* The flowers he selected for his painting were common flowers—they had none of the glamour of Brueghel's rare beauties—and Monet did not strive for the botanical detail that Brueghel had set as his standard; but Monet's painting, which hangs in the Metropolitan Museum of Art in New York, is a joy to all who view it.

Sunflowers became favorite "cottage flowers" in Europe after their arrival from Mexico. Monet cultivated them in his garden at Vétheuil, and they became a frequent subject for his painting. Happily for me, these same Sunflowers, *Helianthus annuus,* grow in profusion in the nearby meadows of northern New Jersey. Other members of the Sunflower family, or even the Black-Eyed Susan, may be used to create an arrangement which will give a similar feeling of form and color. In this arrangement Beech leaves serve as a substitute for the coarse Sunflower foliage.

FLOWERS: From your own garden, or everyone's roadside garden: 16 Sunflowers *(Helianthus annuus)*

FOLIAGE: Beech leaves
CONTAINER: Ceramic vase
MECHANICS: Sand
DECORATION: Oriental-style rug

STEP I Fill container to within an inch of the top with sand.
STEP II Prefabricate sprays of Beech leaves and Sunflowers.
STEP III Arrange.

Flowers in the Order of Their Appearance in the Garden and Along the Roadside

All of the *Plant It Now, Dry It Later* plants appear in "Flowers in the Order of Their Appearance in the Garden and along the Roadside." The latter may be a slightly inappropriate title, for in some of the plants parts other than flowers are useful to the dried bouquet. Some plants, such as Bittersweet and Chinese Lantern, provide fruits; others, such as Honesty and Wheat, provide seeds; and still others, including the Pear and Holly trees, lend their foliage to the dried bouquet. All are labeled as to growth form or duration, whether annuals, biennials, perennials, trees, shrubs, or vines. The time of their flowering, fruiting, or seeding is also noted.

Essentially, then, this is a *Plant It Now, Dry It Later* calendar which will serve as a guide to tell you which plant materials are available for drying at any time during the growing season. It can also help you to plan your garden to produce color when you want it.

The backbone of such a calendar is the flowering trees and shrubs, the bulbs, and the perennial plants whose flowers, fruits, and seeds appear with dependable regularity at approximately the same time year after year. The times noted apply to my garden in northern New Jersey, and there may be variations if your latitude is different from mine. The flowers in a garden south of mine will flower a bit earlier, while in a garden north of mine they will flower a bit later. These variations in flowering times are of minor importance, however. What is important is that the flowering, fruiting, or seeding sequence will be the same regardless of where your garden happens to be.

The annuals and foliage plants have been interspersed throughout the calendar. Most annuals, once in flower, bloom for the rest of the growing season; the commencement of their flowering depends to a large degree on the maturity of the plants. Generally, plants set out in the spring will flower sooner than will plants grown from seed sown at the same time.

Foliage may be gathered from July into fall. Except for those gathered for autumn color I prefer to gather my leaves about the first of August when the new growth has hardened, and before the growing season is too far advanced and the wind, weather, and insects have caused them to deteriorate.

The directions and the time required for processing flowers and foliage are noted. These times are minimal for successful processing and to leave your plant materials in silica gel, or glycerine and water, for longer periods will not hurt them one bit.

FREESIA *(Freesia refracta)* Bulb

Flowers: January to March in my local florist's greenhouse and in the fields of California, and probably in other places I don't know about.

Freesias grow in florists' greenhouses in the east in January and February, and florists without greenhouses have them flown in from California where they are field-grown from November until March. They are among my favorite flowers, not only for their grace but for their sweet fragrance. Freesia is a native of South Africa and is named for the nineteenth-century German botanist Friedrich Heinrich Theodor Freese.

To Dry: It is not necessary to wire Freesia before processing. The flowers are formed along a stem which is easily wired when the flowers are to be used in an arrangement. Hill up some silica gel to accommodate the grace of the spray (page 86). The flowers dry in two days and harden on the stem after four days in silica gel. The white and yellow dry true to color; the orange tones tend to darken.

ACACIA (*Acacia* spp) Tree

Flowers: early spring
Available from florists: mid-February through March

There is considerable confusion about the name of the sprays of clustered, ball-shaped, fluffy yellow flowers often used by florists as a filler for spring bouquets. They are usually referred to incorrectly as Mimosa, but their family name is *Acacia* (Greek for *tree*). *Mimosa* is the name of another family of plants with feathery leaves resembling those of the Acacia. Some members of the *Mimosa* family have leaves that are *touch*-sensitive: they collapse when touched. Acacia leaves are *light* sensitive: they tend to fold as darkness falls.

Acacia has been grown along the Mediterranean and in the Middle East for thousands of years and was the source of the "Shittim wood" of the Old Testament. The trees grace Mediterranean cities today and, when in flower, erupt into fountains of fluffy, butter-yellow balls on branches which cascade like Willows over the sidewalks and streets of Athens. Acacia is grown commercially in California.

To Dry: If hung to dry, Acacia branches will look erect and rather stiff. To achieve a more natural cascading effect, stand the branches on a *kenzan* or needlepoint holder in a shallow bowl of water for four or five days, allowing the water to dry off. As the fluffy balls dry the fluff disappears and the balls become smaller and harder surfaced. They are still very attractive, and hold their color for many months.

PUSSY WILLOW (*Salix discolor*)
Deciduous shrub, wild or cultivated

Flowers: late February and March

Some varieties of this native American shrub are so tall they look like small trees. The catkins, which begin to appear on the sturdy stems in late February, are most luxuriant if the shrub is cut back hard every few years. Pussy Willow is happiest when grown in wet or damp areas, but it does like the sun.

Salix is the Latin word for willow, and willow bark is the natural source of salacin, from which salicylic acid, the principal ingredient of aspirin, is prepared. For centuries the theory prevailed that, if a physical disorder was endemic to an area, the medicinal relief for it would be found growing in the same area—a theory borne out in the case of rheumatic disorders, so prevalent in England, where other Pussy Willows grow in abundance. Salicylates, in synthetic form, are very widely used today in the treatment of rheumatic diseases.

Pussy Willow roots readily when placed in water, which makes it easy to propagate.

To Dry: Cut the stems when the catkins have reached the desired stage of development and stand them dry, in a vase. The catkins can be forced into earlier development if the stems are cut when the catkins first appear and placed in water. Pour the water off when the furry pussies have reached the size you wish.

CROCUS *(Crocus* spp)   Bulb

Flowers: very early in the spring, or in the fall, depending on the species

Spring-Flowering Crocus

Crocus have grown in abundance in Mediterranean countries for thousands of years. The name is Greek for saffron, and this variety provided the yellow dyes associated with the royalty of ancient Greece and provides us with food seasoning today.

The Crocus is the first flower to appear in my garden each spring, a more than welcome sight after a long winter. Late snows often cover the flowers but their hardiness belies their fragile appearance, and as the snows disappear the flowers bloom on. Plant the bulbs two to three inches deep and three and four inches apart. Like other bulbs, the Crocus receives its nourishment through its foliage, so this should not be cut back until it has dried and turned brown.

Spring-Flowering Crocus bloom and are processed in the very early spring when the heat is still on indoors, and I often arrange these flowers under glass as soon as they are thoroughly dry, to avoid the hazards of summer storage of a flower that is more susceptible than most to high summer humidity. If summer storage is a problem, or if you prefer an "open" arrangement of dried Crocus, try some of the autumn-flowering kinds that bloom from September into November: the colorful purple *sativus,* the blue *speciosus,* or the white *speciosus albus.*

To Dry: Crocus open when the sun is full upon them and tend to close when picked and taken indoors. Have your silica gel and wire ready before picking so that little time is lost between picking and processing. Cut the stem near the base. Wire and process in a deep container according to the directions for flowers that are cuplike in form (page 86). Allow seven days for processing. If the natural stem has not fully hardened in that time, loop the wire stem over a wire hanger to complete the drying.

CHRISTMAS ROSE (Helleborus niger)   Perennial

Flowers: late winter

LENTEN ROSE (Helleborus orientalis)

Flowers: mid-April

The Hellebores are among the earliest flowering plants in the garden. Grow the white Christmas Rose for late winter blooming, and the green and purple Lenten Rose to bloom about mid-April. All Hellebores grow best in moist, cool, shady places in a soil to which well-rotted manure should be generously added. They are not fond of moving, so make their position in the garden a permanent one. The plants vary from one to two feet in height and have a beautiful dark green foliage throughout the growing season. During the Middle Ages *Helleborus* was said to be useful as a cathartic and as a cure for gout.

To Dry: Wire and dry for flowers that are cuplike in form (page 86). Allow three days for processing.

Lenten Rose

DOG'S-TOOTH VIOLET (Erythronium americanum)
                                    Perennial Wildflower

ADDER'S TONGUE
TROUT LILY

Flowers: late April, early May

Sometime during the past few centuries "Violet" was added to this flower's common name, Dog's-Tooth, but the flower is not a Violet at all—it is really a Lily.

These are among the most charming of America's native plants. Their family name, *Erythronium,* is Greek and means *red*—something of a misnomer for the yellowish flower in my wildflower garden. This is forgivable, however, when one realizes that the name was assigned to a related European plant (whose flower happens to be a reddish color) long before its American cousins (some of which are red) were discovered.

The flowers appear on stems up to ten inches tall and form an attractive border to the slightly taller Lenten Rose.

To Dry: Use fine wire for the fine-diameter stem. Although the petals are markedly curved, process as directed for flowers that are cuplike in form, page 86. Allow three days.

One of the greatest rewards of drying flowers, it seems to me, is the opportunity to observe, one by one, their many different forms and colors. This is particularly true of the smaller gems of the earth, which are so often overlooked in favor of larger, showier flowers. The small, charming flowers of the hardy bulbs discussed below are not seen in American gardens as often as they should be. Two appear in early spring along with the Crocus; the third blooms as the others fade. Like the Crocus, all are natives of the Mediterranean, and two of them have autumn-flowering relatives.

GLORY-OF-THE-SNOW
(Chionodoxa luciliae and others)   Hardy Bulb
Flowers: early April

Chionodoxa is Greek and means both *snow* and *glory,* a reflection on the early flowering and beauty of these exquisite white, blue, and white, and pink starlike flowers. They are delightful in woodlands and in borders, and often hybridize with *Scilla,* if the two are in close proximity, to produce what is sometimes called *Chionoscilla.* Glory-of-the-Snow was introduced into gardens in 1877 from its home in Crete and Asia Minor.

Siberian Squill

SIBERIAN SQUILL   *(Scilla sibirica* and others)
Hardy Bulb

WILD HYACINTH
BLUE BELL   Hardy Bulb
Flowers: early April

Scilla, Hippocrates' name for this plant, is supposed to mean *I injure—* a reference to the poisonous properties of the bulbs. Don't eat them! Masses of the gentian-blue Siberian Squill in borders, rock gardens, and woodland settings are a sight not soon to be forgotten. The flowers can also be white and pink; they grow quickly and seed themselves freely in almost any soil. The autumn-flowering *Scilla* appears to be a rarity in American gardens.

SNOWFLAKE (*Leucojum* spp)   Hardy Bulb

Flowers: late April–early May

Snowflake

At first glance the bell-like Snowflake looks like Lily-of-the-Valley, but on closer inspection the differences are obvious, particularly in the single spot that appears on each petal of the Snowflake flower. I have seen only green spots, although I understand there are yellow-spotted and reddish-spotted, as well as all-white, relatives. There is also an autumn-flowering cousin, *Leucojum autumnale*.

To Dry: The flower stems of Glory-of-the-Snow and Squill have small diameters and fine wire must be used when wiring them. Process all three as for sprays of flowers, page 86. The flowers dry in three days, but allow five days for the stems to harden. If a part of the stem is still soft when it has been removed from the silica gel, loop the wire stem over a coat hanger to allow it to dry before storing.

DANDELION (*Taraxacum officinale*)   Perennial

Flowers: April and May in quantity: less profusely throughout the growing season

Dandelion

The Dandelion has a large number of relatives, and although I sometimes feel they must all be in my lawn and garden in the spring, only a modest number actually live in the United States. The rest live abroad: in Asia, Europe, and South America. [To the gardener and farmer the appearance of this pretty yellow flower represents extra hours of gardening effort and so its beauty is often lost in the grumblings that accompany the weed pulling and spraying.]

In addition to its tight head of yellow flower, which dries well, the Dandelion plant has food value and medicinal virtues. [My sister-in-law enjoys a salad of young Dandelion leaves served with oil and vinegar, and prefers them to lettuce in a sandwich.] One of the common names of this plant, Piss-a-Bed, which is heard more often in Europe than it is here, attests to the diuretic properties of Dandelion wine and beer.

To Dry: Choose young, fresh flowers. Wire them and dry as for the single flower, page 81. Allow three days for processing.

DAFFODIL (*Narcissus* spp)   Bulb

Flowers: from late April until mid-May, depending on the species

The varied blossoms of the several kinds of these early-flowering bulbs travel under many common names: Daffodil, Jonquil, Paper-

Daffodil

Whites. All dry beautifully and add a fresh note of springtime to the dried bouquet.

[The flower has been so popular that Daffodil exhibitions were held annually in England for many years. Amateur enthusiasts attempting to create new varieties were models of patience, as six to seven years are required from the sowing of the seed to the flowering of the bulb. A new variety shown at the Daffodil Exhibition of 1902 was described as follows: "In the beautiful class of self-yellow trumpet Daffodils the advent of King Alfred marked a great advance—it seems as if hammered out of pure gold." The King Alfred Daffodil is still one of the most popular with home gardeners today, but other kinds should not be overlooked. A browse through a seedsman's fall catalogue will introduce you to short-cup Daffodils, charming poet Narcissi, and Cyclamen-flowered Daffodils which will give great new interest both to your garden and to your dried bouquet. Easy to grow and easy to dry, many of these beauties were among the rare flowers in European gardens in Jan Brueghel's day. Bulbs should be planted in the fall, six inches to 8 inches deep and in more informal distribution than Tulips.]

To Dry: The stems of Daffodils may be wired before or after processing. Whichever you choose to do, cut the stem about one inch below the ovary. Process, trumpet up, as for the single flower, page 81. The trumpet and surrounding petals will be dry in two and a half to three days, but the ovary requires a week in silica gel to dry and harden.

PANSY (*Viola* spp)   Annual or Biennial
Flowers: from early May

"—and there is Pansies, that's for thoughts," said Ophelia to Laertes. Pansy is the English corruption of the French *pensée, thought.* Many of the newer varieties have large, showy, full-faced flowers, but one of my favorites is still the "Johnny Jump-Up" (*Viola tricolor* var. *hortensis*). This miniature pansy-face, which was sprinkled throughout my grandmother's garden beds in early May, reseeds itself readily. The profusion of tiny blue, lilac, and purple faces tinged with yellow and white provide a charming and colorful ground cover among the Tulips. [The "thoughts" which this flower held for young lovers through the centuries are reflected in its older names: Johnny-Jump-Up-and-Kiss-Me, Kiss-Me-behind-the-Garden-Gate, and Cuddle-Me-to-You. It was also known as Hearts-ease, a name probably derived from its medicinal use; according to Gerard, it was recommended "to dissolve inflammations of the breast, lungs, and rough arterie."]

Pansy

Violas and Pansies are perennials, but they are most satisfactory when grown as biennials. Sow the seed after August 1 for flowering the following year. If your winters are unusually severe it may be best to grow them as annuals. Pick Pansies all summer to encourage them to continuous bloom and to prevent them from getting leggy.

To Dry: With the exception of the Johnny Jump-Up, whose full stem I prefer to dry unwired, Pansies may be wired either before or after processing. Process them as for the single flower, page 81, taking care to slip some silica gel between the petals to support the upper petals and retain the natural shape of the flower. The petals are dry to the touch in two days, but I allow five days for processing to permit the stem and other parts of the flower to harden.

DOGWOOD *(Cornus florida)*   Tree or Shrub
Flowers: About mid-May

The Dogwood tree is one of the most beautiful ornamental trees available to the home gardener. Our village is heavily populated with this native of the eastern United States, and in the early spring the trees share their red, pink, and white beauty with us with unbounded generosity.

Forty members of the *Cornus* family live in the temperate regions of the northern hemisphere, but one relative, evidently preferring to be alone, resides in the southern hemisphere, in Peru.

Cornus florida has some interesting uses and virtues. To begin at the source of any plant: its root bark produces a red dye. The tree bark, when powdered, makes a good tooth powder; when mixed with sulfate of iron it produces a good black ink! This same bark has been used as a somewhat less effective substitute for quinine, and it is said that fevers can be allayed by chewing dogwood twigs. The foliage, which turns scarlet in the fall, can be processed in glycerin and water, but it is for its beautiful spring flowers (actually, the colorful bracts which surround the tree's insignificant flowers) that Dogwood is recommended to the gardener or flower arranger.

To Dry: The flowers, on short stems one inch to two inches long, wilt quickly when cut, so they must be processed immediately after picking. Wire and process as for the single flower, page 81, allowing three days for processing.

Checker Lily (or) Gerard's "Checquered Daffodill"

CHECKER LILY *(Fritillaria meleagris)* Bulb

Flowers in early spring

Meleagris, the botanical name for this species, has its roots in the Greek and refers to a guinea hen. Gerard's description would be difficult to improve on: "The Checquered Daffodill, or Ginny-hen Floure, hath small narrow grassie leaves, among which there riseth a stalk three hands high, having at the top 1 or 2 flowers, and sometimes 3, which consisteth of six small leaves checquered most strangely: where in Nature, or rather the creator of all things, hath kept a very wonderful order, surpassing (as in all other things) the curiousest painting that Art can set downe. One square is of a greenish yellow color, the other purple, keeping the same order as well on the backside of the floure as on the inside, although they are blackish in one square, and of a violet color in the other; insomuch that every leaf seemeth to be the feather of a Ginny hen, where of it tooke his name." The flower was greatly esteemed in Gerard's time for the "beautifying of our gardens, and the bosoms of the beautifull."

The culture of *Fritillaria* is similar to that of Freesia: they grow well in Southern California, but, fortunately, they are unlike the latter in that they are hardy in my northern New Jersey latitude. Rabbits seem to be particularly fond of these plants, so it is wise to give them some protection in the garden.

To Dry: Wire and dry as for flowers that are cuplike in form, page 86. When placing the flower in an arrangement, curve the wire stem so that the flower presents its natural pendant or "bell" appearance. Four Days

P. J. Redouté's "Crown Imperial"

CROWN IMPERIAL *(Fritillaria imperialis)*
Hardy Bulb

Flowers: spring

[In 1807 Pierre Joseph Redouté, the French botanical artist, noted with his exquisite drawing of this unusual flower that "it has been known for more than 200 years in the gardens of Europe and it appears to be of the most ancient cultivation. It was first cultivated in Vienna (in Europe) where it had come from the Orient. In general, the choicest of the beautiful ornamental flowers comes to us from the Orient. It flowers in spring."]

The bulb of Crown Imperial is large and is planted, lying on its side, in the fall. "The floures," said Gerard, "grow at the top of the stalk, incompassing it round, in form of an Imperiall crown (whereof it tooke his name) hanging their heads downward as it were bels." The "stalk" is about three feet tall, the flowers either red or yellow.

To Dry: The individual flower stems are short, and the flowers must be processed immediately after picking. Wire and dry as for flowers that are cuplike in form, page 86. Allow four days.

TULIP (*Tulipa* spp) Hardy Bulb
Flowers: mid-April through May

Lily-Flowered Tulips

Tulips graced the gardens of Turkey for centuries before they were introduced into Europe by Busbequius, the Austrian Ambassador to Turkey, who carried some seeds home to Vienna in 1554. A loose Arabic translation of Tulip is *turban,* which describes the shape of this flower nicely.

Tulips are bright spring flowers that cover almost every hue of the spectrum but, curiously, as with several other flowers, avoid blue. Except for some of the bright pinks and reds which dull and darken a bit, most Tulips retain their true color through the drying process. Their forms are varied and interesting. The graceful Lily-Flowered-Tulip, *Tulipa acuminata,* with its pointed petals was a favorite of the gardeners of Turkey. It was obviously among the earliest forms to be cultivated in Europe, for we find it often in Brueghel's early seventeenth-century paintings. Present-day varieties of this Tulip that were grown and dried to recreate Brueghel's *Flowers in a Blue Vase* were the white Triumphator, the yellow Mrs. Moon, and the deep pink Mariette.

The more rounded petal forms such as Her Grace, a Cottage Tulip whose creamy-white petals are edged with rose, Fig. 11, were developed by European horticulturists who evidently preferred curves to angles.

When selecting bulbs for planting and drying I choose different kinds from the early, low-growing *Tulipa kaufmanniana* to the late, tall Darwin, to extend the Tulip season in my garden and to give greater variety to the dried bouquet. Tulips should be planted in clusters or in beds to present the best display. Allow about six inches between the bulbs and plant them at least eight inches deep. Remove the faded flowers before the seed forms if the bulb are expected to flower the following year. Like other bulbs the Tulip feeds through its leaves so these should not be cut back until they have turned brown.

To Dry: Cut the stem as the flower comes into full bloom, never after it has passed its peak of flowering. Process according to directions for flowers that are cuplike in form, page 86. Although the petals are dry in three days, I allow five days for processing to assure a thoroughly dry and hardened stem. Sometimes, if I am hard pressed for the use of the silica gel to process other spring flowers, I use the shorter processing time (three days) and do the following:

1. Melt a bit of paraffin which is kept in a small pan for this purpose.
2. Hold the Tulip upside-down by its bent wire, and with a cotton
   Q-tip apply a bit of the melted paraffin around the base of the
   Tulip.
3. Invert the flower to an upright position, holding it cupped in my
   hand in the desired degree of openness for a few moments to allow the paraffin to harden.
4. Loop the end of the wire stem over a hanger to allow the stem
   to harden before storing.

PHLOX *(Phlox* spp) Perennial

Flowers: in the spring, and July through September, depending on the
species

In April and May the woodlands of the eastern half of North America
are carpeted with the blue of Wild Sweet William *(Phlox divaricata)*.
The plant is also popular with gardeners who grow it in masses with the
taller pink Tulips.

Summer Phlox *(Phlox paniculata)* is one of the few perennial flowers
that provide masses of midsummer color in the garden. The plants flaunt
their showy white, pink, lavender, to red heads from heights of two and
a half to three feet which puts them behind the front row of the sunny
border. They flower best if the roots are generously watered. The more
recently introduced varieties developed by Captain Symons-Jeune, the
English Phlox hybridizer, are especially generous and beautiful in their
summer color, but one of my favorites is a much older variety, Painted
Lady. Its feminine-pink flowers with their burgundy centers dry perfectly true to color, which cannot be said for all of the deeper color kinds.
Although I have not dried the annual Phlox *(Phlox drummondii)* I suspect it, too, should dry well.

To Dry: Either the entire flower head or a segment of the head may be
processed. I cut the stem just below the flower head and stand it in a deep
container for processing. Wire the soft stem of the spring Phlox before
drying, but the stem of summer Phlox is thin and hard and the wiring
may be left until later. The petals are dry in three days but I allow five
days for processing to permit all of the parts of the flower to harden.

MAY APPLE *(Podophyllum peltatum)*
Perennial wildflower

Flowers: April through May

May Apple is a native plant of the United States. The other members of the *Podophyllum* family reside in China and the Himalayas. The family name is a shortened form of *Anapodophyllum* which means "duck's-foot-leaf"—a descriptive phrase which attests to the fanciful imagination of the botanist who named it! May Apple is a low-growing, shady-woodland plant whose lone white flower nods beneath the one to three palm-lobed leaves. Its fragrance is nauseously sweet, but this is lost in the drying process. The plant is sometimes referred to, erroneously, as Mandrake, but the real Mandrake, which was sought after by Old World romantics for its root which supposedly resembled a human form and purportedly had aphrodisiac properties, is *Mandragora*.

To Dry: Wire and process as for the single flower, page 81, allowing three days for processing.

AZALEA *(Rhododendron* spp)   Shrub
RHODODENDRON

Flowers: Early spring through June, depending on the species

Azaleas and Rhododendrons are members of the same family, and although it is a simple matter to distinguish between the two in my garden, botanists tell me that in the higher altitudes of western China and the Himalayas, where most of these gorgeous, ornamental shrubs grow in great profusion, to sort them out is a highly technical matter.

Horticulturists sort the plants as deciduous Azaleas, evergreen Azaleas, and evergreen Rhododendrons. About sixteen of the 350 known members of the Rhododendron family are native to the United States, and most of these are the deciduous Azalea kind. One of the best known is the Pinxter-Flower *(Rhododendron nudiflorum)* whose pink blooms appear about the time of Pentecost. The early Pennsylvania Dutch settlers who discovered the plant associated its blooming with this religious period and called it, in their German, *Pfingsten*, of which Pinxter is a corruption. Two other early-blooming, hardy, deciduous native plants are the pink Royal Azalea, *Rhododendron schlippenbachi,* and the purple *Rhododendron mucronulatum*. The Mollis, Ghent, Knaphill, and Exbury Azaleas are hardy, deciduous hybrids whose flowers are lovely shades of red, orange, yellow, pink, and white.

The Indian Azaleas that are not hardy in the north, and the Japanese Kurume Azaleas, which do survive the winter in my garden, as well as

Rhododendron

the plants which gardeners refer to as Rhododendron, are all evergreen plants. All prefer an acid soil and, except for some of the hybrid sorts, partial shade.

To Dry: Single flowers, sprays of flowers, or flower clusters are simple to process. Single flowers may be wired or not, and dried as directed for flowers that are cuplike in form, page 86; allow three days. Process the sprays as directed on page 86; allow four days. Cluster heads of the larger flowers present a somewhat greater challenge. The stems of some kinds of Rhododendron are hard and woody and are sometimes difficult to wire. I prefer to cut these stems about two inches below the flower cluster, leaving further lengthening until the flower is to be arranged. Stand the stem in the silica gel and process for flowers that are cuplike in form, page 86. Allow one week for all parts to harden. Most colors dry true, but some of the shades of red and purple become dull during the processing.

Evergreen Rhododendron foliage may be processed in glycerin and water, page 90. It may be possible to preserve the deciduous foliage, too, although I have not experimented with it.

ALKANET (Anchusa officinalis) Perennial
BUGLOSS

Flowers: April and May in my garden

Alkanet

Because of their small size, the flowers of *Anchusa* which resemble Forget-Me-Nots, are one of the more easily overlooked flowers in Brueghel's *Flowers in a Blue Vase.*

"The cups of the floures are of a skie colour tending to purple," said Gerard. I find these mounds of bright blue flowers to be especially pleasing under white-flowering Dogwood.

Anchousa, from which this plant derived its name, means *a paint for the skin* and refers to the root. "The root," Gerard goes on to say, "is a finger thicke, the pith or inner part thereof is of a wooddie substance, dying the hands or whatsoever toucheth the same, of a bloudie colour."

To Dry: Cut the stem below the flower head. Wire with fine wire and dry as for the single flower, page 81. Allow three days.

BRIDAL WREATH (*Spiraea* spp)   Shrub
BRIDEWORT
QUEEN'S NEEDLEWORK
Flowers: Late spring and early summer depending on the species

Two sorts of Bridal Wreath grow in my garden. Both are immigrants to the United States, having left their homes in the area that spans Eastern Europe to the Himalayas and Northeastern Asia. The tiny, white parasol-like flowers of *Spiraea arguta* burst into bloom all along the shrub's stiff, twiggy branches early in May. In slight contrast, mounds of clustered white flowers appear like tiny bouquets along the soft, graceful new growth of *Spiraea vanhouttei* early in June. It is easy to imagine how sprays of the latter were entwined to make garlands and wreaths to adorn June brides in bygone days!

Bridal Wreath grows well in sun and ordinary soil. *Spiraea arguta* is grown most often as a single specimen; *Spiraea vanhouttei* is frequently grown in rows as hedges and property dividers.

To Dry: Cut the sprays *as the flowers come into bloom.* Process as directed for sprays of flowers, page 86. Allow three days.

Bridal Wreath *(Spiraea vanhouttei)*

PRIMROSE (*Primula* spp)   Perennial
Flowers: In the spring

In April the great shaggy cows of Normandy enjoy a special treat as the river banks and the roadside drainage ditches become awash with yellow Cowslip, one of the best-known of the *Primula* family. The *Primulas* became a favorite plant for plant hunters in China and the Himalayas where the climate at the higher altitudes most closely approximates that of Europe, thereby assuring the greatest success in transplanting most of the 225 oriental members of this large family to occidental gardens. Robert Furber featured many of these exotic spring-flowering plants in his garden catalogue, *Twelve Months of Flowers,* in 1730.

Primrose is low growing and produces heads of clustered flowers on stems that rise above flat leaves. Except as potted plants the flowers are rarely seen indoors in their fresh state. Dried, however, they add a new dimension to indoor floral decoration.

Primrose

To Dry: Nip the flower stem an inch or two below the flower head. Wire and dry as for the single flower, page 81. Allow four days.

REDBUD *(Cercis canadensis)*   Tree
Flowers: Early in May in my garden

I think one of the most refreshing sights of spring anywhere is in the restored English colony of Williamsburg, Virginia, when the Redbud is in flower. The trees are often planted beside the white picket fences that protect the Colonial gardens, and as the flowers erupt in their rosy-purple clusters all along the leafless branches it is a sight to behold! A variety, *alba,* has white flowers.

Only two kinds of Redbud are dependably hardy in my northern New Jersey garden: the Eastern native, *Cercis canadensis,* and its somewhat less hardy Chinese cousin, *Cercis chinensis.* Both are beautiful ornamental shrubs or small trees for the smaller property. Other equally attractive species are hardy further south.

To Dry: I have dried *Cercis canadensis* successfully, and suspect the other should dry well, too. Cut the twigs as the flowers approach their peak of bloom. Process as directed for sprays of flowers, page 86; allow four days.

ROCK CRESS *(Arabis alpina)*   Perennial
Flowers: Mid-May

Rock Cress provides a charming and freely spreading border to the spring garden. Its many low spikes of pink or white flowers remind one of a miniature Stock, and they arrive with the Dogwood, Violets, and Azaleas. The plants are of easy culture and do well in rock gardens and wall niches. It is particularly delightful to grow near the kitchen door if the exposure there is a sunny one so you can see and enjoy this herald of spring most often.

Redbud

To Dry: Wire and dry as for the single flower, page 81. Allow three days for processing.

WILD GERANIUM *(Geranium* spp)
CRANE'S BILL   Perennial—wild or cultivated
Flowers: Spring through summer depending on the species

Unlike our popular bedding Geraniums that trace their ancestry to the native South African *Pelargoniums,* the true Geraniums have relatives all around the world. America's garden takes on an additional international flavor with the planting of cultivated varieties from the

Iberian Peninsula *(Geranium ibericum)* and the Dalmation Coast *(Geranium dalmaticum)*. Of the many natives to the United States my favorite for the wildflower garden is *Geranium maculatum (maculatum* means spotted), whose charming, spotted, pinkish-lavender flowers appear in my garden in the spring and early summer.

Depending on the species, the Geraniums vary in color from pale pink through the lavenders to blue-violet, and in height grow from a dwarfish four inches to two feet. Depending on the species, some are sun-loving while others prefer shade.

To Dry: The Geraniums wilt within a matter of minutes after being picked, and it is necessary to have a water supply near at hand if the flowers are to be expected to retain their fresh appearance for drying. Either single flowers or sprays of flowers may be dried. Wire and dry both as for the single flower, page 81. Allow three days for the single flower, four days for the spray.

GLOBEFLOWER *(Trollius* sp)   Perennial

Flowers: mid-May to midsummer, depending on species

Globeflowers give the appearance of great buttercups during the day, but at night the petals fold to golden globes, hence their popular name. The flowers rise on stems above a mound of green foliage to stand about two feet tall. Species of Globeflower are native to Scotland and Siberia, which guarantees them to be plants hardy in cold climates. Plant in dampish places for the best growth.

To Dry: Wire and dry in silica gel as for the flower that is cuplike in form, page 86. The petals are dry to the touch in three days but allow four days if possible. *Trollius* is one of five *Plant It Now, Dry It Later* flower families that have petaloid sepals and, therefore, have no calyx supporting their "petals." The additional day of processing is helpful in hardening the stem behind the flower.

RANUNCULUS *(Ranunculus asiaticus)*   Tender corn

Flowers: January–February in my local florist garden
May–June in gardens further south

Most of the almost 300 members of the Ranunculus family live in temperate climate zones. A few stragglers have moved farther north into cooler regions while a few others have preferred the higher temperatures of the tropics. Our popular garden and florist Ranunculuses have their parentage in the beautiful *Ranunculus asiaticus* which is native to Iran

(Persia). The oversized Buttercup-shaped flowers (they often exceed two inches in diameter) are formed on stems reminiscent of those of the Anemone. They fluctuate widely in petal number and, in color, cover every hue of the spectrum but for some reason skip over the blue. The Ranunculus was one of the rare flowers which Jan Brueghel included in his early seventeenth-century paintings. Although it is freely cultivated in California it does not appear nearly as often as it should in East Coast gardens.

To Dry: Wire and dry, following directions for flowers that are cuplike in form, page 86. Allow four days for processing.

HAWTHORN *(Crataegus oxycantha* var. *paulii)*   Tree
Flowers: Late May

The storied hedgerows of rural England are often the thorny Hawthorn, *Crataegus oxycantha,* and in May the country lanes are edged in their lacy, white blossoms.

There are many species of Hawthorn and the color of their blossoms varies from white to pink and red. Paul's Double Scarlet, *Crataegus oxycantha* var. *paulii,* is the Hawthorn in my garden and in late May clusters of scarlet flowers, nestled against fresh green leaves, burst into bloom, turning the tree into a showpiece of color.

All Hawthorns, including the many native American species, bloom only in the spring with the exception of the Glastonbury thorn, *Crataegus biflora.* This tree has its sire at the Glastonbury Abbey in England where, according to Christian legend, the Holy Grail was brought by Joseph of Arimathea after the death of Christ. Joseph is supposed to have thrust his staff into the earth at Glastonbury, whereupon it took root to become the thorn to which the Abbey later lent its name. For many years the tree is alleged to have bloomed on Christmas Day as well as in the spring. In our gardens it blooms late in the fall, and irregularly in the early spring, but not at Christmastime.

The wood of the Hawthorn is very hard and tough, and this characteristic is the basis for its family name, *Crataegus,* which is derived from the Greek word, *Kratos,* meaning *strength.*

To Dry: The flower clusters are short stemmed, and I usually process them as for the single flower, page 81, for use in small arrangements. Larger sprays may be processed according to their expected use and the availability of the silica gel, following the directions for processing sprays, page 86. Allow four days for processing.

HEATH (*Erica* spp)   Evergreen Shrubs
and
HEATHER (*Calluna vulgaris*)

The names Heath and Heather are often used interchangeably and although the two plants bear a strong resemblance to each other they actually refer to two plant families, not one.

The major difference between them is that the Heath (*Erica*) derives its color from the corolla of the flower while the Heather (*Calluna*) gains its color from the calyx. However, their common characteristics are many: Both are spikey, dwarf plants with a liking for full sun, poor soil, and exposure to most kinds of weather. They require almost no care and are free of insects and diseases. Carefully selected and planted, Heath and Heather will give color to the garden for most months of the year.

HEATH (*Erica* spp)
Flowers: Most months depending on species

There are about 500 members of the *Erica* family; some 470 of them live in South Africa and the rest trail northward through Africa, the Mediterranean, and Europe where the northermost relatives live in Norway. South Africa became a plant hunter's paradise after it was colonized by the British in 1820, and for the next quarter century each new *Erica* to arrive in England created a wave of excitement among English plant lovers equaled only by the waves the plants themselves must have endured as they sailed north from the South African ports.

Only a few members of the *Erica* family are hardy as far north as my New Jersey garden, but their colors are lovely: shades of pink, bright rosy-reds and white.

HEATHER (*Calluna vulgaris*)
Flowers: depends on the variety

Unlike the very large Heath genus, the Heather genus has but a single member which inhabits Asia Minor and western and northern Europe. Like many of our ancestors, it sailed westward across the Atlantic and has become naturalized in eastern North America. *Calluna* means to *sweep* in Greek, a comment on the use to which the evergreen spikes were put in an earlier day. The flowers are pink to rosy red, and sometimes white.

To Dry: Cut the stems of both Heath and Heather as the flowers near their peak of color and hang.

GUELDER ROSE (*Viburnum opulus* var. *sterilis*)
SNOWBALL TREE   Shrub
Flowers: May and June

There are many species and varieties of Viburnum, but I find the deciduous Snowball Tree of China and Japan, *Viburnum opulus* var. *sterilis,* of greatest interest in the garden and in the dried bouquet. It grows easily to fifteen feet in sun or light shade, and in May and June is covered with rounded white flower clusters that resemble the Hydrangea in form, although the two plants are only distantly related.

To Dry: Pick when the flower heads are fresh and the single flowers are crisp to the touch. The stems of the heads are very short, so leave as much stem as possible when cutting. Wire, and dry, either as for the single flower, page 81, or as for flower clusters on sturdy stems, page 86. Allow three days for processing.

PEONY (*Paeonia* spp)   Perennial and Treelike Shrubs
Flowers: Tree, mid-May
Perennial, about Memorial Day

China has been called the "Mother of Gardens," and certainly she has earned this title of parenthood when one considers the vast number of her native plants such as the Asters, Chrysanthemums, Peonies, and Azaleas that reside in our American gardens. My favorite of these natives of China are the magnificent Peonies whose name in Chinese is *moutan.* They are also among the most sensational flowers for use in the dried bouquet. Drying does not dull the petals and these six-inch to eight-inch beauties retain an unbelievably fresh appearance through the drying process, Fig. 11.

Most of our herbaceous garden Peonies seem to have their ancestry in the European *Paeonia officinalis* and/or the *Paeonia albiflora* which has been cultivated in China for almost 2500 years. The Tree Peony (*Paeonia moutan)* is a relative newcomer to Chinese horticultural history: its cultivation has been known for only 1200 years. Western travelers to China 100 years ago reported some 250 varieties of Peony ranging in color

Peony

from white, yellow, red, blue, to nearly black (a very dark maroon). The herbaceous Peonies are often set in rows and were used to edge walks and flower beds in old-fashioned gardens.

The Tree Peony flowers about two weeks earlier than the herbaceous Peony. Once established in the garden it demands little attention and prefers to have its roots left undisturbed. It requires no pruning and asks only that its open situation in the garden be provided with some protection for its buds against late spring frost. Although it makes remarkably few demands on its owner, the Tree Peony is a plant overwhelmingly generous in its beauty, producing its magnificent flowers year after year. Tree Peonies are somewhat more expensive than the herbaceous Peonies but they are an investment never to be regretted.

To Dry: The blooms of the Peonies are so large that a separate container is usually required to process each one. Wire, and dry as for flowers that are cuplike in form, page 86. Allow three days for processing.

SWEET ROCKET
DAME'S VIOLET *(Hesperis matronalis)* Perennial
DAMASK VIOLET

Flowers: From early June into August

As with many plants, such as the Ox-Eye Daisy, which, today, we look upon as weeds, Sweet Rocket arrived in America with the early colonists who grew it in their gardens. According to Gerard, "The distilled water of the floures hereof is counted to be a most effectuall thing to procure sweat." Unfortunately, he offers no further details regarding the distillation process but perhaps this was common knowledge at that time. It, too, thrived on both sides of colonial garden fences but, while the Daisy has lost favor as a cultivated plant, Sweet Rocket in both its single and double forms has survived as a favorite of American gardeners. The original plant had single flowers of four petals each, but Gerard reported in 1635 that "By the industrie of some of our florists within this two or three years hath beene brought to our knowledge a very beautiful kind of these Dame Violets, having very faire double white floures."

Today, both the single and double flowers appear in lovely shades of pink through purple, and white, in clustered heads that look a bit like Phlox. The stems reach a height of three feet. The family name, *Hesperis*, refers to *evening* which is when the fragrance of these sweet-smelling flowers is greatest.

Gerard's "Dame's Violets"

To Dry: Wire and dry the flower cluster as for the single flower, page 81. Allow three days.

COLUMBINE *(Aquilegia vulgaris)*   Perennial

Flowers: May and June

The thirty or so species of Columbine that have reseeded themselves for centuries all around the northern hemisphere are among the gardener's favorite early summer flowers. *Aquilegia vulgaris* is the parent of most of our garden Columbine, and these range in color from pale pink through purple, and include blue and white. Our native red and yellow Columbine, *Aquilegia canadensis,* is found growing in much of the eastern two-thirds of the United States and Canada. In the interest of preserving our wild flowers I confine my drying to the garden varieties.

Columbine was "used especially to decke the gardens of the curious" in the seventeenth century, according to Gerard, who described the flower as having "five little hornes, as it were hanging forth, with small leaves standing upright of the shape of little birds."

To Dry: Columbine is one of several flowers that combine the characteristics of both the single flower and the flower that is cuplike in form. In addition, it has the "hornes" or spurs. Hill up some silica gel as for the single flower, page 81, and then make a depression in the hill to accommodate the spurs. I do not wire these longer flower stems until I am ready to arrange them. Drying takes three days.

Gerard's "Red Columbine"

LILAC *(Syringa* spp)   Deciduous Shrub

Flowers: Mid-May into June depending on the species

Lilacs have resided in American gardens for so many years that most of us have forgotten that they are not our native plants but have migrated from their homelands that extend from Southeastern Europe eastward to the Himalayas, and on to Northern China, Korea, and Japan. They arrived first in Vienna from Turkey about the middle of the sixteenth century bearing a Turkish name that likened the flower cluster to a fox's tail!

Many varieties of single- and double-flowering Lilacs are available to American gardeners in a parade of colors that range from deep purple to blue-lavender, rose, pink, white and, more recently, pale yellow. The common single-flowered Lilac is the most fragrant but the flowers of the double-flowered kinds last longer. All prefer sun and a well-drained soil.

When growing Lilacs as a hedge, plant all of the same kind to reinforce their common habit of growth and color for the best appearance.

To Dry: Process as directed for flower clusters on sturdy stems, page 86. Allow three days.

GERANIUM (Pelargonium zonale) Shrub, usually grown as an annual

I often marvel at the imagination of the ancient Greeks who could liken the shape of a flower and/or its fruit to a creature of the land, sea, or air. Snapdragon, whose botanical name, *Antirrhinum,* means *dragon snout;* Delphinium *(dolphin);* and now Geranium, which means *crane,* a commentary on the resemblance of the fruit to a crane's bill. We can go one step further: *Pelargonium* means *stork—*is further comment necessary? The ancestors of our cheery potting and bedding Geraniums were natives of the Cape of Good Hope that migrated to England aboard sailing vessels about 1710, and since that time hybridizers have created many varieties of this garden favorite. I plant them, in masses, in my garden about Memorial Day, and they bloom on and on until nipped by frost. Geraniums are easy to grow in average soil and should be set in the sun for maximum bloom. For stocky, bushier plants press the ground firmly around the plant when transplanting.

Geranium

To Dry: Not all of the single flowers that compose the flower cluster open at the same time, and to prevent those which open first (the ones on top) from becoming detached in the processing the flower cluster must be picked while some of the lower flowers are still in bud.

Cut the stem an inch below the cluster. Wire and dry as for the single flower, page 81. Allow four days for all parts to harden. Both the pinks and the reds retain their natural colors beautifully.

ROSE (Rosa spp) Shrub

Flowers: From June until frost

"The Rose," said Gerard, "though it be a shrub full of prickles, doth deserve the chiefest and most principall place among all floures."

Obviously, Gerard appreciated the beauty of the Roses in his garden, and it is with a sense of regret that we realize that he was unable to experience the beauty of our Hybrid Teas such as Peace and Tropicana. However, the ancestor of these garden favorites, *Rosa odorata,* a double flower of blush color that had the fragrance of tea, would not make the hazardous sea voyage around Cape Horn in its migration from China to Europe until 1810. Other native Roses of East Asia that grace today's gardens are the Polyanthas, of which my favorite is the Fairy, and the popular Rambler Roses.

The Rose has been under cultivation for so many centuries that its origins have been lost in the dim recesses of the horticultural history of China and the Middle East. The pagans believed that all Roses were white until the dripping blood of Venus dyed some of them red. The story of the

Gerard's "The white Rose"

consuming passion of the mighty warrior Mars for Venus, who preferred the younger Adonis, is both romantic and tragic. Mars killed Adonis in the hope that Venus would forget her young lover and return to him. The story continues that as Venus ran to the aid of Adonis, she stepped on a thorn and fell onto some white-flowering Rosebushes where blood from the thorn-prick turned some of the Roses red.

It is beyond the scope of *Plant It Now, Dry It Later* to discuss the horticulture of Roses, a topic which has already filled many volumes. It is germane only to say that many kinds of Roses—Tea Roses, Floribundas, Grandiflora, Polyanthas, and others—can be dried for months of enjoyment.

Among my own favorites for garden planting and drying are:

Name	Kind	Color
Queen Elizabeth	Grandiflora	shell pink
Betty Prior	Floribunda	deep rose
Garden Party	Hybrid Tea	creamy white tinged with pink
Tiffany	Hybrid Tea	pink
Radiance	Hybrid Tea	pink
Chicago Peace	Hybrid Tea	pink
King's Ransom	Hybrid Tea	yellow
Ma Perkins	Floribunda	pink
Maman Cochet	Hybrid Tea	salmon pink
The Doctor	Hybrid Tea	pink
Tropicana	Hybrid Tea	bright red-orange
Montezuma	Grandiflora	bright salmon pink
Virgo	Hybrid Tea	white
The Fairy	Polyantha	pink

To Dry: A single flower, a spray of Polyanthas, or a corsage of Roses may be dried. Directions for selecting and processing are on page 84. With the exception of the deep reds, which darken, all colors appear to dry true. Rose foliage may also be dried. See Foliage, page 93.

IRIS (*Iris* spp)   Perennial
Flowers: May and June

Iris is Greek for *rainbow* and I do not think there is another word that could serve as a more appropriate name for these flowers that touch on every hue of the spectrum.

The Iris are all natives of the North Temperate Zone and have been cultivated for so many tens of centuries that there seems to be no agreement among botanists as to how many truly native kinds there really are, although the number is probably between 140 and 170.

Gerard's "Germane Floure de-luce"

The popular German Iris of our gardens *(Iris germanica)* is not native to the United States but, rather, its home belts the area between Central Europe and North Africa eastward to China. The flower has been widely used to grace the Mohammedan "Cities of the Dead," which may partially account for its wide cultivation and distribution in the Middle East.

The roots of the German Iris, when grown in a loose, rocky, mountain soil, have a fragrance of Violets, and are known as Orrisroot (actually, "Iris root"), "whereof sweet waters, sweet powders, and such are made," to quote Gerard.

All Iris, whether German, Japanese *(Iris kaempferi)*, or Siberian *(Iris sibirica)* are easy to grow, multiply freely and are beautiful in the garden.

To Dry: Iris are not recommended for drying in areas where summer humidity exceeds seventy percent. The petals of the flower are more fragile after they have been dried and the moisture has been removed from them than when they were fresh, and it is only with the greatest of difficulty that they retain their form during storage.

Wire and dry as for the single flower, page 81. Allow seven days. Particular caution must be taken when spilling the silica gel from the dried flower to avoid tearing them.

CHIVE *(Allium schoenoprasum)*   Perennial
Flowers: June

This perennial herb belongs to the onion family. Its slender, hollow leaves, when cut fine, are used to flavor soups, salads, vegetables, and meats. Its pinkish-lavender flowers appear on the plant in June. Chive does not reseed itself, and the plant should be divided early each spring for propagation.

To Dry: Cut the stems at their base before the flowers are fully open. Hang to dry.

Chive

MAIDENHAIR FERN   *(Adiantum* spp)   Perennial or Pot
Plant in my latitude depending on the species
Foliage

These exquisite ferns may have been a favorite of your grandmother or great-grandmother in the days when it was fashionable to cultivate ferns indoors in cabinets.

The only member of the Maidenhair Fern family that is hardly in my garden is *Adiantum pedatum* which thrives best in a moist, well-drained soil in a partly shaded place in the garden. The new fronds are a bright, springy green which darken as the summer advances. For drying, these

Maidenhair Fern

Clematis

Ferns should be gathered early in the season when their color is brightest.

Many of the other members of this family that are grown in pots in northern New Jersey are hardly outdoors in the warmer climates of the western hemisphere—from the southern United States and Bermuda through the Caribbean where they cascade along the roadside in Fern Valley in Jamaica, into Brazil, Bolivia and Peru, and on south into Chile. Maidenhair Ferns also grow up and down the East coast of Asia. The kind most often available in pots from the florist is *Adiantum cuneatum*, which is a native of Trinidad. All those I have processed dry beautifully.

To Dry: See Processing Maidenhair Fern, page 93.

CLEMATIS (*Clematis* spp)   Vine
Flowers: From early June depending on variety

The Clematis (the Greek *kiema* refers to *climbing*) is one of the most elegant of plants, and has yet to find its deserved popularity in American gardens.

Most members of the Clematis family are hardy, rapid climbers which require support. Their leafstalks have the curious habit of entwining themselves around anything with which they come in contact—whether it happens to be another leafstalk or a plant support. *Clematis jackmanii* the large-flowered purple Clematis developed in 1862 by George Jackman, climbs my garden fence while Mme. Baron-Veillard, a mauvy pink, entwines its flowering arms around my circular, brownstone garden house.

Clematis is virtually unseen in fresh flower arrangements because of its short stems and viney habit of growth, and so it adds a new dimension to the dried bouquet.

To Dry: The flower stem is short, fine, and sometimes difficult to thread with a wire. I find it easier, when cutting, to leave the longest stem possible, and add the necessary length of wire later when the flower is to be used. Process as for the single flower, p. 81, allowing three days in silica gel. The purple *Clematis jackmanii* becomes a beautiful blue during the processing. All other colors remain true.

FEVERFEW (*Chrysanthemum parthenium*) MATRICARIA
Flowers: In profusion in June; in lesser quantity in the fall

Feverfew is an old-fashioned plant whose home covers much of Europe and extends as far east as the Caucasus. For centuries Europeans attributed many medicinal virtues to this plant, which probably accounts for its early arrival in America. Feverfew is a corruption of "Febrifuge," which indicates the antipyretic properties ascribed to the plant in years gone by. Another of its common names, Matricaria, is derived from the Latin *Mater (mother)* and *caries (decay),* and refers to its medicinal use in diseases of the uterus.

The small, white Daisy-like flowers with their yellow centers are formed in flat clusters on rather bushy plants that grow from one foot to 3 feet tall. Although Feverfew is most commonly seen as a single flower, I prefer the double varieties as a background for the more outstanding and colorful flowers in the early summer garden and for use as a filler in the dried bouquet.

To Dry: Process as directed for flower clusters on sturdy stems, page 86. Allow three days for processing.

WHEAT *(Triticum aestivum)*   Annual grass
Flowers: Mid-June

Wheat seems too important to me to be considered an annual grass, but that is just what it is. My source of supply is rather modest, for in northern New Jersey Wheat is not grown over vast acres of farmland as it is in the Midwest; rather, it springs up unannounced, in fields or along a sunny stretch of roadside where, perhaps, its seed has been dropped by birds as they travel from one backyard bird feeder to another. If the maintenance crews of our local road departments are dilatory in the spring application of their herbicides, the Wheat is ripe and ready for picking about the middle of June. Not only is Wheat interesting in the dried bouquet, but its hollow stem can be used to provide added stem length for other dried materials. See "About Stems," page 110.

To Dry: Simply cut the stems near the ground and stand them in a tall vase until they are needed.

OX-EYE DAISY *(Chrysanthemum leucanthemum)*
Perennial wildflower
Flowers: In profusion in June; in lesser numbers until October

Although it is not a native plant, the Ox-Eye Daisy is one of the prettiest of America's wildflowers. It has its home in Europe and Northern Asia and arrived here with the early settlers who grew it in their gardens, probably for its medicinal virtues. "The floures of Oxie eie made up in

Ox-Eye Daisy

seare-cloth doe assuage and waste away cold hard swellings," wrote Gerard, quoting Dioscorides, "and it is reported that if they be drunk by and by after bathing, they make them in short time well coloured that have been troubled with the yellow jaundice."

The plants are prolific in their reseeding and the one- to three-foot-tall plants often appear, unannounced but not unwelcome, in my garden. The flowers grace meadows and roadsides in profusion in early June and are often gathered by the pailsful to decorate church altars on Children's Day.

To Dry: Wire and dry as for the single flower on page 81, allowing three days.

PAINTED DAISY	*(Chrysanthemum coccineum)*
	or
INSECT POWDER PLANT	*(Pyrethrum roseum* in older writings)*
	Perennial

Flowers: Mid-June in my garden

The Painted Daisy Plant is conservative in its branching and in the number of flowers it produces, but this native of the Caucasus and Iran more than makes up for the lack of quantity in the quality of its blooms. The single and double flowers look truly like Daisies painted in luscious shades of crimson, pink, rose, and lilac. Some are tipped with yellow but the flowers are never completely yellow, nor do they ever appear in blue. The white flower closely resembles the Shasta Daisy. The plants grow from one foot to two feet tall. Their display in the garden will be enhanced if several plants are set together.

Its other common name, Insect Powder Plant, seems strange for so pretty a flower, but the plant has been grown in France and California for use in the preparation of the insecticide powder, pyrethrum.

To Dry: Wire and dry as for the single flower, page 81. Allow three days.

Painted Daisy

XERANTHEMUM   (Xeranthemum annuum)   Annual

Xeranthemum is one of the many flowers that have never acquired popular English names, and so it continues to be known by its botanical name which is Greek and means *dry flower*. The plant is a native of southern Europe and is easily grown from seed in our American gardens. It attains a height of two feet and produces many attractive, Daisy-like everlasting flowers about an inch and a half in diameter, with satiny petals that range in color from white through the pinks to purple. The plants flower from July until frost in my garden.

To Dry: Cut the stems before the flowers have fully opened; bundle and hang to dry. I sometimes wire the flowers at a more open stage of development and process them in silica gel for twenty-four hours which helps the petals to retain their satiny appearance and eliminates the small shrinkage which they undergo when hung.

QUEEN ANNE'S LACE   (Daucus carota)
WILD CARROT
BIRD'S NEST   Biennial wildflower

Flowers: From mid-June through August

Queen Anne's Lace

The lace that Queen Anne wore has long been forgotten, but each summer we are reminded of its gentle fragility by this flower to which it must have borne a resemblance.

This is one of several flowers which I call "railroad weeds"—Ironweed and Tansy being others—because of their proliferation along our local abandoned railroad right-of-ways. At maturity, the slightly convex head of small, white flowers (with an anomalous purplish one dead-center) rides atop a sturdy stem which can grow as tall as five feet. When immature, and again when the flowers have passed, the flower heads form a concave cluster which resembles a bird's nest, giving another common name to this wild beauty.

To Dry: Cut the stems near the base, choosing flowers in varying stages of development for maximum arrangement interest. Dry according to directions for flower clusters on sturdy stems, page 86. The flower heads are dry in two days but should be left for four days to hasten the hardening of the stem just below the flower head.

GLOBE THISTLE   (Echinops sp)   Perennial
Flowers: Mid-June to mid-July, and again in the fall

Globe Thistle has been a European favorite for centuries and bunches of the dried flowers are sold in the city markets in late summer and fall. It is a robust and delightful plant for the back of the sunny border. Dependable and disease free, the relatively low foliage sends forth sturdy stalks up to six feet tall in June and again in late summer. Each stalk is

Globe Thistle

topped with a spiked, steel-blue globe. The plant is an interesting and attractive background for Shasta Daisies and the early lemon yellow Yarrow, *Achillea taygetea*, which bloom at the same time in June. Globe Thistle grows best if it is divided every two or three years. Through division, the single plant which I set out in my garden ten years ago is now many, and in the gardens of friends.

To Dry: Cut the stalks to any desired length when the globe has begun to turn blue but before the flower spikes have opened. Tie four or five stalks together and hang to dry. The attic in the heat of summer should be avoided as a place for drying as the globe heads tend to deteriorate and break apart if they are dried too rapidly. Properly dried, Globe Thistle will give years of pleasure in the dried bouquet.

I sometimes create additional interest for an arrangement by drying Globe Thistle in silica gel when some of the flower spikes have opened. The flower heads are processed according to the directions for flower clusters on sturdy stems, page 86, allowing two days for the processing. They may be stored by standing in a vase.

SEA HOLLY *(Eryngium amethystinum)* Perennial
Flowers: June into August

Falstaff's "kissing comfits" are reported to have been the candied roots of Sea Holly. It is not for the supposed aphrodisiac and restorative powers of its roots that Sea Holly is of interest to us today, but rather for its metallic blue and amethyst-toned Teasel-like flowers that appear on sturdy two- to three-foot stems through the summer months.

Sea Holly is a favorite seashore plant, which means that it grows best in sun and sandy soil. Other attractive kinds grow inland.

To Dry: The stems may be cut and hung to dry but a more natural appearance will be retained if the flower head is placed in silica gel for two days. See "Processing Flower Clusters on Sturdy Stems," page 86.

DELPHINIUM *(Delphinium* spp) Annual or Perennial
LARKSPUR
DOLPHIN-FLOWER
KNIGHT'S SPURS
Flowers: The annuals through the summer; the perennials in June and again in late summer

Larkspur and Delphinium are look-alike members of the same family, but the Larkspur is an annual plant and the Delphinium a perennial.

The plant's popular names, Dolphin-Flower and Knight's Spurs, are a reflection of the culture and imagination of the local populace in the various parts of the North Temperate Zone where these plants have their home.

The annual Larkspur *(Delphinium ajacis)* produces its beautiful flowers in feminine pinks, lavenders, blues, and white on three- to five-foot stalks. The plants are easy to grow from seed although the germination is slow—usually twenty days. Larkspur does not transplant easily, so the tiny seeds should be mixed with a little sand and broadcast, early in the growing season, over the area where the plants are expected to bloom. Thin the plants to stand eighteen inches apart when they are two feet tall.

Most of the garden varieties of the perennial *Delphinium* have their ancestry in three other members of this family of some sixty relatives: *Delphinium grandiflorium,* which arrived from Siberia about 1880, *Delphinium formosum,* and *Delphinium hybridum.* The flowers range along the three- to eight-foot stalks in colors that travel all through the blues to purple, and white. The flower spikes should be cut before the flowers go to seed if the plants are to be expected to bloom again in August and September. Divide the roots every two or three years to assure the largest and most beautiful blooms; a dressing of well-rotted manure in the late fall will assure the most vigorous growth. Both the annual and perennial plants should be grown in full sun.

Larkspur

To Dry: Either the individual flower or an entire flower spike may be dried. The single flower may be wired or not, depending on its intended use, and dried as for the single flower, page 86. Allow three days.

When drying an entire flower spike, cut the stalk just below the bottom flower, and dry according to the directions for stalks of flowers, page 86. Allow four days. The remainder of the stalk may be laid aside to dry and harden for use later to lengthen the shortened stalk. See "About Stems," page 110, for other ways to extend the stem when you are ready to arrange your dried Delphinium.

BLACK-EYED SUSAN *(Rudbeckia hirta)* Perennial
Flowers: Summer into fall

Carl von Linné was the eldest son of a Swedish country minister. His efforts to follow in his father's footsteps were disastrous, and in 1729 he transferred to Uppsala College to study medicine which, at that time, was primarily a study of botany. Carl was a poor boy but he was an enthusiastic student, and his potential was recognized by Olaf Rudbeck, Professor of Botany. Professor Rudbeck invited him to live in the Rudbeck home,

Black-Eyed Susan

share the library, and earn his way by tutoring some of the twenty-four Rudbeck children. When Linnaeus, as von Linné was later to be known, devised his modern system for naming all plant life, he honored his former professor by giving his name to this popular cone flower.

The wind or a passing bird may have been your benefactor if this lovely Daisy-like perennial has appeared, uninvited, in your garden. If you have not been so blessed, try the cultivated varieties, which include the yellow-centered Gloriosa Daisy, that are available from seedsmen and nurserymen. The plants do best in sun or very light shade. They are prolific bloomers and a single plant will provide many flowers for fresh or dry bouquets.

To Dry: Stand the freshly cut stems in water overnight to be assured of firm petals and the best flower form. Process in silica gel as for the single flower, page 81. Allow three days for processing.

I often wonder what geological accidents have been responsible for the geographical distribution of plants, particularly in the case of Everlastings, for more of these are native to Australia and South Africa than anywhere else in the world. Seeds of Acroclinium and Rhodanthe, two of the sixty-odd members of the *Helipterum* family endemic to these continents, are available to the American home gardener. These herbs are charming in the garden and in the small bouquet. In Greek, *Helipterum* means *sun* and *wing*, which helps to describe the Daisy-like appearance of these flowers.

ACROCLINIUM   *(Helipterum roseum)*
Annual in my garden; Perennial further south

Acroclinium is a low-growing plant (rarely exceeding fifteen inches in height) which, like other Everlastings, thrives best in a sunny situation in the garden. When fully opened the double and semi-double flowers are approximately two inches in diameter. Non-gardening flower enthusiasts will find bunches of these flowers in jewel-like tones of bright pink, pale pink, chamois, and white at the florist in the fall.

To Dry: Cut the stems before the flowers reach their peak of maturity. Bundle and hang to allow the stems to harden.

RHODANTHE *(Helipterum manglesii)*

Annual in my garden

SWAN RIVER EVERLASTING   Perennial further south

Flowers: Late June

Rhodanthus means *rose-flowered,* and the feminine pink flowers of Captain Mangles' Rhodanthe nod their heads on the slender stems of these fragile-looking plants. Originally, the flowers were pink only, but they now range from deep red to white, and include a pale yellow. Rhodanthe does not create an outstanding display in the garden, and the plant rarely exceeds eighteen inches in height, but this charming Daisy-shaped flower is my favorite among the Everlastings. Rhodanthe is recommended for pot gardening, although its flowering is of rather short duration and continuous bloom should not be expected.

Rhodanthe

To Dry: Cut the individual stems or the plant stem near the base when most of the flowers have opened. I lay these in a box until the stems have hardened, as hanging tends to straighten the stems, causing the flowers to lose their graceful nodding appearance.

POPPY *(Papaver* spp)

The Poppies are among the most brilliantly colored of our garden flowers, but they are almost never seen indoors because of the very short duration of their flowering. In my dry garden, however, Poppies bloom for years!

Three of the Poppies recommended to the *Plant It Now, Dry It Later* gardener have their homes in Europe and the Eastern Mediterranean. The fourth, the Iceland Poppy, is an Arctic cousin, as one might surmise from its name.

CORN POPPY *(Papaver rhoeas)*   Annual

From the fields of Flanders to the Mediterranean the Corn Poppy has run wild over Europe. The garlands of Poppies and Corn that adorn the statues of Ceres, the Goddess of Agriculture, are a wry commentary on how freely these exquisite flowers must have reseeded themselves in ancient cornfields to the undoubted exasperation of ancient farmers. The cheerful single and double Shirley Poppies, whose seeds are so readily

Opium Poppy

available to the American gardener, are a variety of the Corn Poppy. The flowers emerge from their nodding buds in a spectrum of color on stems that attain a height of a foot and a half. The plants do best when planted in full sun in any respectable garden soil.

OPIUM POPPY *(Papaver somniferum)*   Annual

> Not Poppy, nor Mandragora
> Nor all the drowsy syrups of the world
> Shall ever medicine thee to that sweet sleep
> Which thou ow'dst yesterday.
>
> *(Othello,* III-3)

Iago's Poppy of Sleep was once among the most common of garden Poppies, but this tall beauty has declined in popularity, partly because it drops its petals so quickly that it is totally useless as a cut flower. Toward the end of the sixteenth century ornamental varieties of the Opium Poppy began to arrive in Europe from Constantinople. "Pink Beauty," a double, salmon-pink, Peony-flowered variety, is outstanding in the garden and in the dried bouquet.

Oriental Poppy

ORIENTAL POPPY *(Papaver orientale)*   Perennial

Flowers: May and June

The largest of Poppies riding on the tallest of stems are the hardy Oriental Poppies. Their colors range mostly through the reds, from pink to orange. Once established in the garden these plants increase in their beauty as years go by.

ICELAND POPPY *(Papaver nudicaule)*   Perennial

(But I usually grow it as an annual)

Flowers: In the summer

The hardiness of this native of Siberia makes the Iceland Poppy particularly well adapted to northern gardens. The plants are not so tall as the other Poppies—they range in height from one foot to one and a half feet—but the brightly colored yellow, orange, red, and white flowers are sure to delight the gardeners who grow them.

To Dry: Cut the stems in the early morning when the flowers are young. Stand them in water for an hour or two, then wire and process for flowers that are cuplike in form, page 86. Allow three days. The white, yellow, orange, and some pink Poppies dry true to color. Other pinks, as well as the brilliant reds, tend to become a dull shade of old rose.

LAVENDER (*Lavandula* sp)   Perennial

Flowers: Mid-June well into July and again in September

Lavender

> Lavender, sweet Lavender,
> Who'll buy my sweet Lavender?

The Lavender girl of eighteenth century London probably gave little thought to where her sweet Lavender had come from as she offered "Two bunches a penny, Sweet Lavender!" Even today we speak of *English* Lavender as if it were a native plant of the British Isles, when, in reality, it was carried there by the Romans from its home in southern Europe. The family name, *Lavandula,* is derived from the Latin, *lava,* which means *to wash,* a reference to the age-old use of the bruised flowers and foliage to perfume the bath. The popularity of the refreshing fragrance of Lavender has not diminished through the centuries, and today the distilled oil of the flowers is used in the preparation of soaps, perfumes, and other products.

A variety of only one of the twenty or so species of Lavender is dependably hardy as far north as my garden. Hidcote Lavender, a variety of uncertain species, was developed at the beautiful English gardens of Hidcote Manor in Gloucestershire where it borders the walk in the Pillar Garden and flowers with Mock Orange *(Philadelphus lemoinei)* in early summer. Mature plants send forth hundreds of foot-tall spikes of lovely, deep blue-purple flowers that perfume the air. Lavender is partial to sun and a dry, slightly limed soil. Lavender "Hidcote," as it is sometimes called, is available from most nurserymen.

To Dry: Cut the spikes carefully. Tie them in small bundles and hang where it is warm and dark. The dried Lavender loses its purple in the drying process but you will have a lovely, deep blue flower to add to your dry garden.

If you enjoy the fresh fragrance of Lavender in linens or lingerie, pack the crushed flowers in sachets for your own, or your friends', enjoyment.

DAY LILY (*Hemerocallis* spp)   Perennial

Flowers: early June to September, depending on variety

Lemon Lily

It is a tribute to the adaptability of many plants that, within a broad latitudinal range, they can be transported from one area of the world to another, often with widely varying soil conditions, and continue to flourish. Such is the case of the best known of the Day Lilies, the yellow Lemon Lily *(Hemerocallis flava),* a native of northern Europe, which has made itself at home over almost the entire length and breadth of our land.

Day Lilies are seldom seen indoors because of the sequential one-day flowering of the buds which are clustered at the top of the two- to-four-foot stalks. When the Lemon Lilies are used as cut flowers, however, their sweet fragrance perfumes the room in which they stand.

Newer varieties, such as the apricot-colored Colonial Dame, and the pink Mary Anne, have widened the color range of the Day Lilies. Flowering times vary, too, and with careful selection Day Lilies can provide garden color throughout most of the growing season. All Day Lilies are satisfactory garden plants. They have a careless concern for heat and cold, or whether their roots are wet or dry. They are pest-free and require virtually no care. The only attention they ask is to be divided every two or three years. Treat the roots to a good dose of manure when replanting.

The most common of all Day Lilies to the northeastern United States is the Orange Day Lily, *Hemerocallis fulva,* which is found in abundance along river banks and roadsides. It dries as well as the garden varieties, but I do not recommend it for the dried bouquet because Day Lily colors that border on the orange tend to darken to an unattractive brown during the drying process.

To Dry: The branch supporting the individual flower is short, and so the Day Lily must be processed immediately after picking. Nip the flower branch, wire, and dry in silica gel for four days, following the directions for flowers that are cuplike in form on page 86.

YARROW (*Achillea* spp) Perennial
MILFOIL Wild and cultivated

Flowers: June until September, depending on variety

Yarrow, sometimes called "the commonest kind of a weed," has been finding increasing favor with home gardeners, particularly those who appreciate its use in the dried bouquet. One of its common names, *Milfoil,* means *thousand leaves* and refers to the finely cut foliage of the plant. Its botanical name, *Achillea,* honors Achilles, the hero of the Trojan Wars, who is reported to have used the healing properties of the herb to treat the wounds of his soldiers.

The plants thrive in sun and poor soil—to give them too much water is to threaten them with extinction. Depending on the variety, Yarrow may be found blooming from early June until September. I particularly like the lemon yellow *Achillea tagetea* which grows to about one and a half feet tall and is at its best in June. Coronation Gold and Gold Plate grow taller—from three to five feet—and produce their flower heads on sturdy stems in July and August.

Yarrow

To Dry: The flower head is rather large and slightly convex and is composed of many tiny flowers. All Yarrows may be hung to dry but the most natural appearance of *Achillea tagetea* and the white roadside Yarrow *(Achillea lanulosa)* is retained if they are processed for two days in silica gel, following the directions for flower clusters on sturdy stems, page 86. *Achillea lanulosa* retains its best appearance if picked before mid-July. *Achillea millefolium,* whose named varieties include Cerise Queen and Rose Beauty, is the cerise-toned Yarrow so colorful in the garden. It tends to lose its blush to become a less attractive purple when processed in silica gel. Also, its stem is not as stiff as other varieties, and it must be hung after processing to allow the stem under the flower head to harden. Coronation Gold and Gold Plate need only to be cut at the peak of their flowering, bundled, and hung until ready for use. Bunches of these latter varieties are available from the florist in the fall.

BELL FLOWER, BALLOON FLOWER
(Platycodon grandiflorum)   Perennial
Flowers: June into September

In the early botanical sorting of plants the pretty Bell Flower was thought to be a relative of the Canterbury Bell, and so it was assigned to the *Campanula* family. It was not until 1830 that it was recognized as comprising a separate family which seems to have only one member. Its botanical name, *Platycodon,* is from the Greek *platys* which means *broad,* and *kodon,* meaning *bell,* which immediately distinguishes the flower from the more slender Canterbury Bell. The flowers appear along stems of rather sparse foliage, and they are either blue or white, or sometimes blue *and* white. The plants grow to two feet tall, prefer a medium sandy soil that is well-drained, and do well in sun or very light shade.

Platycodon is native to the Far East where it grows wild in Japan, Korea, Siberia, and China.

To Dry: Each flower has a stiff stem up to four inches long and so it is not necessary to wire the flower before processing. Process as for a flower that is cuplike in form, page 86, allowing four days for processing. When using the Bell Flower in arrangements I usually prefabricate the stems to recreate the natural growing habit of the flowers, although they may be used individually in an arrangement if that is preferred.

CANDYTUFT (*Iberis* spp)   Annual and Perennial

Flowers: The annual, through the summer; The perennial, in the spring and early summer

Spain lent her ancient name, Iberia, to these annual and perennial plants whose white and colored tufts appear on stems six inches to eighteen inches tall, depending on the species. Candytufts are not native to Spain alone, however; they are also found growing along southern Europe, northern Africa and eastward to western Asia. The first Candytuft introduced into gardens was the annual kind with the colored flowers, *Iberis umbellata*, which was a native of Candia—hence its popular name. The white annual is *Iberis amara;* the white perennial answers to the name *Iberis sempervirens.* All grow well in sunny, dry places.

To Dry: Cut the stem an inch below the tuft of flowers. Wire and dry as for the single flower, page 81. Allow three days. I sometimes assemble several of these tufts to form a larger, more dramatic cluster for an arrangement.

SHASTA DAISY (*Chrysanthemum maximum*) Perennial

Flowers: In profusion in early summer in my garden; in lesser numbers in the fall

The large, snow-white single and double blooms of the Shasta Daisies are a perfect foil for other flowers, whether in the garden or in the dried bouquet. Its garden beauty multiplies and the finest flowers are assured if the plants are divided every two or three years. Plant them in full sun, allowing about one foot between the plants.

To Dry: Wire and dry as for the single flower, page 81. Allow three days.

LILY (*Lilium* spp)   Hardy Bulb

Flowers: June through August, depending on the kind

"The [white] Lillie," said Gerard, "is called in Latine, *Lilium*, and also *Juno's* Rose, because as it is reported it came up of her milke that fell upon the ground. For the Poets feigne, That *Hercules*, who *Jupiter* had by *Alcumena*, was put to *Juno's* breasts whilest shee was asleepe; and after the sucking there fell away aboundance of milke, and that one part was spilt in the heavens, and the other on the earth, and that of this sprang the Lilly, and of the other the circle in the heavens called the milky way."

In addition to the approximately 100 native Lilies that grow all around the northern hemisphere, including the "white Lillie" in Gerard's garden *(Lilium candidum)*, there is an indefinite number of hybrids available to the American home gardener. Some are funnel-shaped, some bell-shaped, while the petals of others such as the Turk's Cap Lily *(Lilium martagon)* curl back upon themselves. All are beautiful and interesting additions to the summer garden.

To Dry: Wire and dry as for flowers that are cuplike in form, page 86. Allow seven days. I cannot predict the drying results of all Lilies except to say that *Lilium candidum* dries beautifully and remains sparkling white. *Lilium martagon* also dries well but the bright red-oranges dull considerably. Experiment with your own favorites to determine their drying results.

EVERLASTINGS IN THE LOCAL FLORIST GARDEN

There are two Everlastings that do not grow in the United States but which are imported from other lands, and these are available from the florist in the fall. They are very attractive and much sought after for home decoration, and you may enjoy knowing their names and something about them:

SKYROCKET *(Syngonanthus elegans)*

The popular Portuguese name for this tiny flower is *sempre-viva*, which means *live forever*, and it grows in the sandy meadows in the higher altitudes in Brazil. The plant is a low rosette of leaves which sends forth many stiff, slender stems about a foot and a half tall. Each stem is topped with a tiny natural-colored, strawlike flower. The flowers appear during the rainy season, and gathering them is an off-season occupation for Brazilian villagers who then lay them along the roadside to dry. They are later bundled and shipped to Brazilian port cities where many are dyed in beautiful decorator colors to appear later at the florist's. These flowers are attractive when used alone or in small clusters in a mixed bouquet.

IMMORTELLE
YELLOW EVERLASTING *(Helichrysum arenarium)*

Immortelle (Fig. 1) is popular in the *bouquet sec* in France, where this foot-tall perennial with its white wooly stem and foliage grows well in sand. The clustered flowers are chrome-yellow, strawlike globes about the size of a large pea. They are sometimes bleached white and then dyed burnt orange, green, red, and blue. The bleached and dyed colors are available in limited quantities in the United States but my own preference is for the natural yellow color which is the one that is most available to us. They are extremely durable in both color and form, and with their heads massed tightly together they are used to make the crosses and wreathes that provide winter decoration in the churches of southern France.

Anemone

ANEMONE *(Anemone coronaria)* Tender Bulb (Corm) WINDFLOWER

Flowers: Eight to ten weeks after bulb is planted in my garden

In April and May the brilliant purples and reds of the giant Anemone de Caen burst forth from the rich, moist earth of Normandy, while their ancestors, the smaller Poppy Anemone, *Anemone coronaria,* enliven the countryside of the Holy Land. In Greek *anemos* means *wind,* which accounts for the popular name of Windflower, and at one time it was thought that these "Lilies-of-the-Field" bloomed only when the wind blew.

In milder climates Anemone corms can be planted in the fall and the plants grown as perennials, but in my garden the corms do not survive the cold of winter, and so I grow them as annuals, planting the corms early each spring in partial shade, and lifting them each fall. The pink to red, blue to purple, and white flowers appear eight to ten weeks after planting.

The giant Anemone de Caen, grown in the fields of California, and elsewhere in greenhouses, are available from the florist from October through April.

To Dry: Cut the stem one-half inch below the flower, wire and dry as for flowers that are cuplike in form, page 86. For a more natural appearance cut one-half inch below the stem foliage, wire and dry, upright, in a tin deep enough to accommodate the added stem length. Allow four days for all parts to harden.

HYDRANGEA *(Hydrangea macrophylla)* Shrub
Flowers: Summer through fall

Water vessel is the meaning of the Greek name of this beautiful ornamental shrub, a reference to the cuplike shape of its fruit.

There are about thirty-five members of the *Hydrangea* family but it is from *Hydrangea macrophylla* (*macrophylla* means *large-leaved*) that most of our showy pink- and blue-flowered varieties have been developed. In varying degrees these flowers have the curious ability to shift their colors depending on the acidity or alkalinity of the soil in which they grow. The plants first arrived in England from their native China and Japan in 1790, and one can imagine the utter consternation of the London gardener of 1800 who planted a pink-flowered Hydrangea only to have it produce blue blooms! It was not until 1821 that someone discovered that aluminum in the soil would change the flower color from pink to blue.

Hydrangea flowers most freely when grown in full sun, but they must be assured of an ample water supply to quench their summer thirst.

To Dry: Either the entire flower head or a part of it may be processed. The primary flower heads are often too large for use indoors and so I prefer to dry the smaller, secondary blooms which appear beneath the main flower. Process as directed for flower clusters on sturdy stems, page 86. Allow three days.

PURPLE PLUM (*Prunus cerasifera* var. *pissardii*)   Tree

Foliage: From mid-June

Prunus, Pine, and Bamboo are the three friends of Chinese floral art, and they appear together over and over again on ancient and modern porcelain dishes and bowls, and on bottles and jars.

The *Prunus* family includes Almond, Cherry, Peach, and Plum. All are hardy, small ornamental trees for the garden or lawn. I have processed the foliage of only one, *Prunus cerasifera* var. *pissardii*, and its lovely, deep purple-bronze foliage has become one of my favorites for the dried bouquet.

To Dry: Process in glycerin and water, page 90.

PASSIONFLOWER (*Passiflora caerulea*)   Tender Perennial Vine

Flowers: Through the year in the greenhouses of Northern New Jersey

The Passionflower, whose intriguing religious interpretation originated with the early Spanish explorers who discovered the flowering plant draped like garlands from the trees in its native habitat in tropical and subtropical America, is still something of a curiosity in our local greenhouses. I have included it here for the benefit of those who may find it available, both for its interest to the dried bouquet, and for study.

The Spaniards read into the flower's components the passion of Jesus Christ and interpreted their discovery as a sign to convert the Indians to Christianity. The flower and its miraculous interpretation caused waves of excitement among the Christian hierarchy in Rome where Jacomo Bosio was doing an exhaustive study on the Cross of Calvary. He included the following in his writings in 1610:

> The flower represents not so directly the Cross of our Lord as the past mysteries of the Passion. It is a native of the Indies, of Peru, and of New Spain, where the Spaniards call it "the Flower of the Five Wounds," and it had clearly been designed by the great Creator that it might, in due time, assist in the conversion of the heathen among whom it grows. The upper petals are tawny in Peru, but in New Spain they are white, tinged with rose. The filaments above resemble a blood-coloured fringe, as though suggesting the scourge with which our blessed Lord was tormented. The column rises in the middle. The nails are above it; the crown of thorns encircles the column; and close in the center of the flower are five spots or stains of the hue of blood, evidently setting forth the five wounds received by our Lord on the Cross. The crown itself is surrounded by a kind of veil, or very fine hair, of a violet colour, the filaments of which number seventy-two, answering to the number of thorns with which, according to tradition, our Lord's crown was set; and the leaves of the plant, abundant and beautiful, are shaped like the head of a lance or pike, referring, no doubt, to that which pierced the side of our Savior, whilst they are marked beneath with round spots, signifying the thirty pieces of silver.

The Passionflower was available to European gardeners by the early eighteenth century and was featured in the September arrangement of Furber's *Twelve Months of Flowers*.

To Dry: Wire and dry as for the single flower, page 81. Allow three days. The flower sometimes fades a bit during the processing but is still very interesting for arrangements or for study. Individual leaves may also be dried in silica gel in the same manner. Allow three days.

Passionflower

DUSTY MILLER *(Artemisia stelleriana)* Perennial
ARTEMISIA
WORMWOOD
OLD WOMAN
Foliage

It is sometimes amusing to speculate about the common names that plants have acquired, and I wonder if the silvery white down that covers the leaves of this plant resembled, in bygone days, a miller covered with flour dust at the end of his day's work. However romantic our ideas might be about names, it is for its lovely "dusty" foliage that this plant is attractive in the garden and in the dried bouquet. Of the many members of this large family, the two-foot-tall *Artemisia stelleriana,* found in the mid-Atlantic states but native to northeast Asia, appears to be most useful for planting and drying. The plant survives in the most ordinary of soils and requires little attention, asking only for a sunny situation in the garden. Other members of the large *Artemisia* family have been cultivated since ancient times for their medicinal virtues. Absinthe, for example, is derived from *Artemisia absinthium,* and santonica, used as an anthelmintic, is a derivative of the oriental *Artemisia cina.*

To Dry: Artemisia may be hung to dry, but a softer effect will be achieved if it is processed in silica gel for two days before storing.

SCOTCH BROOM *(Cytisus scoparius)* Shrub
Foliage

Scotch Broom is sought after by flower arrangers for the graceful line which its sprays of sparse foliage can be encouraged to assume.

The plant, which grows to ten feet tall, is a native of Europe and the Far East, but has become naturalized in the eastern part of the United States and in the Pacific Northwest. It is rather indifferent to the soil in which it stands and is often found in dry, waste places.

Sprays of Scotch Broom are available at the florist's from spring through fall.

To Dry: Cut and hang. If a particular curve is desired, wrap a fresh spray with enameled wire, bow to the desired arc, and string a wire between the ends until the spray has dried.

SNOW-ON-THE-MOUNTAIN *(Euphorbia marginata)*
Annual

MILKWEED
GHOSTWEED
Foliage

King Juba of Mauritania is supposed to have named this plant family after his physician, Euphorbos.

"The sap or liquor that is extracted out of this plant," said Gerard, "is of the colour and substance of the Creame of Milke; it burneth the mouth extremely, and the dust or powder doth very much annoy the head and the parts thereabout, causing great and vehement sneezing, and stuffing of all the pores." A real irritant for the eyes, mouth, nose, or open sores!

Snow-on-the-Mountain is a two-foot-tall native American foliage plant whose light green leaves, the upper ones margined in white (or sometimes all white), are a refreshing sight in the sunny border. They present this same refreshing appearance in the dried bouquet.

To Dry: Process the sprays of Snow-on-the-Mountain as for sprays of flowers, page 86. The leaves are dry in three days but allow five days for the stems to harden.

SUMMER SALVIA *(Salvia farinacea)*   Annual

Salvia is the ancient Latin word meaning *to be healthy*, which is a reflection of the medicinal virtues ascribed to some of the 500 members of the *Salvia* family. The virtues of the Summer Salvia, however, are in its beauty in the garden and in the dried bouquet. The bushy plants form many two-foot-tall spikes of tiny flowers, ranging in color from white, and white tinged with blue, through blue to purple. Planted in rows, or as individual specimens in the sunny border or bed, the colors are a foil for almost all other summer garden flowers. I grow the plants as annuals, but they are considered to be half-hardy perennials, and often winter over in my garden if covered with a mulch.

To Dry: Cut the stems near the ground. Bundle and hang to dry. If you choose, dry the stems in silica gel for two days to retard petal shrinkage before hanging.

STOKE'S ASTER *(Stokesia laevis)* Perennial
STOKESIA

Flowers: From mid-July

Stokesia became an American contribution to English and Continental gardens after James Gordon, the London nurseryman, found the plant growing in South Carolina in 1766. It is also native to Georgia and Louisiana, but it has had no difficulty in making itself at home in my garden, where it has bloomed faithfully for years.

The flower is sometimes described as being similar to an Aster in appearance. Its color is reminiscent of a China-blue touched with lavender, and the center is white. The color does not change through the drying process. The petals open during the day and tend to close at night. Stokesia is low-growing and belongs in the front of the sunny border.

To Dry: Wire and dry as for the single flower, page 81. Although the petals are dry to the touch in two days, I usually allow four days for processing because of the tendency of the flower to close during storage if processed for the shorter time. Actually, the flower is pretty either way, and the variety of full and partially opened flowers will add interest to your bouquet.

CARNATION *(Dianthus* spp) Annual and Perennial
PINK

Flowers: In the summer in my garden

John Gerard called the Carnations and Pinks in his seventeenth-century London garden "Gillofloures." On their hardiness he commented: "[The Carnation Gillofloures] are kept in pots from the extremity of our cold winters" but "the Clove Gillofloure (or Pinke) endureth better the cold, and therefore is planted in gardens."

Carnations and Pinks were cultivated in Greece more than 2000 years ago along with Iris, Roses, and Narcissus. The original flower was pink, but by the sixteenth century the color had been broken into its red and white components by enthusiastic gardeners in England, France, Italy, Holland, and Germany. Indeed, so many new varieties were developed that Gerard was caused to comment "to describe each would be to roll Sisyphus'* stone, or to number the sands."

Gerard's "great double Carnation"

---

*In mythology, Sisyphus was the evil King of Corinth whose eternal punishment in Hades was to push a heavy stone up a hill only to have it roll down each time.

There are many charming Carnations and Pinks available to the home gardener and those who choose to pick their flowers at the florist's. They range in color from red through pink to lavender, pink and white, red and white, and white, although the red is so dominant that one rarely sees a white flower without a speck of red.

To Dry: All flowers undergo some shrinkage as the moisture is drawn from them, and this is particularly evident in the case of the Carnation where the petals become very loose in the receptacle when dry. It is necessary, then, to twist a wire around the throat of the receptacle to be assured that the petals remain firmly in position. Wire and dry as for the single flower, page 81. Allow three days. Some colors undergo a change during processing. However, with the exception of the deeper rose tones of the Pinks, which become dull and darken considerably, most are attractive.

Twisting wire about throat of receptacle

WINGED EVERLASTING *(Ammobium alatum)*
Annual

Ammobium, as I prefer to call this small white Daisy-like everlasting with a yellow center, is not a sensational flower in the garden. The self-branching stems are leggy and resemble the stems of Statice but they are not so stiff. They grow to heights of three feet, and each is crowned with a small white flower which looks out of proportion to the height of the stem and its thickness. However, when dried and arranged in clusters, "Winged Everlasting," as it is popularly called, adds a fresh note of white and an interesting variation of form and texture to the dried bouquet. Its name means *to live in sand,* which should help you to place this native of Australia properly in your garden.

To Dry: The flowers can be picked, bundled, and hung to dry from mid-summer through light frost. If cut before the yellow center shows, the effect will be pure white. If cut after the center has appeared the final effect is white "petals" around a darkened center. Even when dry, the stems are never really stiff, and so I add a length of wire before wrapping the stems together when prefabricating them for arrangements.

Winged Everlasting

ORNAMENTAL GRASSES (various families)

The Place du Vieux-Marché in Rouen, centuries-old capital of Upper Normandy, bursts into bloom each morning as the farmers and their wives bring their flowers to market in the great open square. In April their pails are filled with giant Anemone, Ranunculus, Freesia, and other bright blooms to be sold before the statue of Joan of Arc, on the spot where the Maid of Orléans was burned at the stake in 1431. They are a beautiful daily tribute to the young girl who inspired the forces of Charles VII to victory over the English during the Hundred Years' War.

Just a few steps from this old market place, on the Rue du Gros Horlage, I stepped into a small tidy seed shop. Behind the marble counters one sees in the cities of Normandy, the proprietors in their gray frockcoats stood ready to serve the customer.

The seeds were identified by the pictures on their brightly colored packages, and I scanned the racks to find those useful for the *bouquet sec.* One of my selections was not prepackaged, however, and the proprietor carefully weighed out ten grams of seed, slipped them into a large packet, and added the label GRAMINÉES ORNEMENTALES EN MÉLANGE. *"En mélange,"* to be sure, for I counted eighteen varieties of ornamental grass seed! A sunny corner of the garden was prepared, the seed planted, and it was with eager anticipation that I looked forward to their harvest to learn just what it was I had purchased.

Never disappointed with any harvest, I was amused to find Quaking Grass *(Briza maxima),* Job's Tears *(Coix lacryma-jobi),* and other old familiar favorites—one more proof that the home gardener need not travel this wide world to find garden variety!

To Dry: Grasses require no processing for use in the dried bouquet. Simply cut and stand in a jar or vase until needed.

HONESTY *(Lunaria annua)*   Biennial
Seeds: Late July–early August

Has any other humble plant been graced with so many common names? *Lunaria* is derived from the Latin *luna* which means *moon,* a comment on the shape of the seed pod, which is so useful to the dried bouquet. In England it is known as Moonwart, and in France as *Herbe aux Lunettes (eyeglass plant).* In the United States it answers to the names of Peter's Penny, Silver Dollar, and Money Plant.

Honesty requires little attention in the garden and readily reseeds itself. The two-and-a-half- to three-foot plants produce lavender-colored flowers of little consequence in early summer which are followed by the flat, slightly ovaled seed pods.

To Dry: Cut the stalk late in July or early August when the seed pods appear to be bone dry, and before old age and the weather have caused them to deteriorate. Rub each flat pod gently but firmly between the thumb and forefinger to remove the dried outer surfaces of the seed pod,

Gerard's "White Sattin floure" (Honesty)

thereby exposing the useful silvery partition of the seed vessel. Your Honesty is ready for immediate use or may be set aside in a tall container until needed.

FLOWERING CRABAPPLE (*Malus* sp)   Tree
Foliage: From mid-July

This is one of a group of magnificent small ornamental trees that had its origin in China, although its family name, *Malus,* is the Greek word for apple. It is not for its blossoms that turn it into a pink spectacle in the springtime that the Flowering Crab is useful to the dried bouquet, but rather for its foliage, which becomes a beautiful bronzy-green during the processing while retaining its natural form and suppleness.

To Dry: Cut the branches to eighteen inches in length. Process in glycerin and water, following the directions on page 90. The processing is usually completed within three days.

MOUNTAIN LAUREL (*Kalmia latifolia*)   Shrub
Foliage

Mountain Laurel

The Laurels, our beautiful ornamental evergreens, are American natives whose Latin name, *Kalmia,* honors Peter Kalm, a Swedish botanist who traveled and collected plants in North America in the mid-eighteenth century.

Mountain Laurel is much sought after as a landscape plant for its clusters of beautiful white, pink, or purple flowers which arrive in the spring, and for its shiny evergreen foliage. It is this foliage which, when processed, I find useful to the dried bouquet.

The shrubs prefer a partially shaded place in the garden but will do well in sun if provided with sufficient moisture. Except for clay, the plants do well in most kinds of soil but, like other popular broadleaf evergreens, they have an intense dislike of limestone.

To Dry: Process in glycerin and water, page 90.

CALENDULA (*Calendula officinalis*)   Annual
The "Marygold" of Shakespeare's day was the flower we now call the Calendula. The colors vary from creamy-white through soft yellows to apricot. If the dead flowers and seed heads are cut from the plant it will provide continuous bloom throughout the growing season. Grow this beauty in the sun, allowing about twelve inches between plants. In

California the Calendula, often called Pot Marigold, is frequently used as a bedding plant. The flower is beautiful when arranged either fresh or dried.

To Dry: Wire and dry in silica gel as for the single flower, page 81. Allow five days for processing.

BELLS OF IRELAND *(Moluccella laevis)*   Annual

This interesting green "flower" was a great favorite in old-fashioned gardens where it was known as Shellflower. Whether it is called Shells or Bells, it is from the shape of the calyx that it derives its name rather than from the insignificant whitish flowers that nestle within them.

Bells of Ireland are of easy culture and if you are growing them for the first time you will be fascinated, as I was, to observe the Bells as they develop along almost the entire length of the stem. This is an interesting plant for the border and for the dried bouquet. Bells of Ireland are available from the florist in time to celebrate St. Patrick's Day in March and again in early fall.

To Dry: Cut the stem near the base and remove the foliage. Remove any Bells that have yellowed (the oldest ones near the base of the stem), and process for five days according to directions for sprays of flowers, page 86. If the stem has not hardened completely, lay the spray in a box until the stem is firm. I usually touch the base of each Bell with a bit of melted paraffin to secure its position along the stem.

MAGNOLIA *(Magnolia grandiflora)*   Tree
BULL BAY
Foliage

If China is truly the "Mother of Gardens," then the eastern coast of the United States must be her offspring, for the flowering plants of China have more in common with this part of our country than anywhere else in the northern hemisphere. In fact, a surprising number of plants, and the Magnolia is one, are native to these two areas of the world only, and are found nowhere else! In a flight of fancy, one can imagine a Chinese Johnny Appleseed, his pockets filled with seeds, digging the proverbial hole to the other side of the world, to spread the beauty of China's flowering plants!

Of the thirty-five members of this family, it is the magnificent, broadleafed evergreen *Magnolia grandiflora*, whose foliage becomes a rich chocolate brown during processing, that is most useful to the dried bou-

Magnolia

quet. This tree can be grown as far north as Philadelphia if it is planted where it can avoid most of the winter snows that would otherwise lay heavy on the leaves and cause the weighted branches to break. Sprays of Magnolia leaves are available from the florist during many months of the year.

To Dry: Process in glycerin and water as directed on page 90.

BOXWOOD *(Buxus japonica)* Shrub
Foliage

"The Box tree," wrote Gerard, "groweth greene winter and summer, the leaves bee round, and of a light greene." English Boxwood is not dependably hardy in northern New Jersey, but its Oriental relative, *Buxus japonica,* is hardy north into Canada, and it is this kind that grows in my garden. The shrub has many branches of lustrous leaves that are somewhat more oval than the English kind. It is very slow-growing, eventually attaining a maximum height of six feet.

Boxwood is not particular in its horticulture demands except for its preference for a well-drained soil and a bit of shade.

To Dry: Process in glycerin and water, page 90.

Gerard's "The Box tree"

PEAR *(Pyrus communis)* Tree
Foliage

"The tame Peare trees," wrote Gerard, "are planted in Orchards, as be the Apple trees, and by grafting, though upon wilde stockes, come much varietie of good and pleasant fruits."

It might surprise Gerard as well as the farmers of Southern Europe and Asia who have cultivated the Pear since ancient times to learn that its foliage, when processed, is one of the most attractive for use in the dried bouquet.

To Dry: Process in glycerin and water, page 90.

Gerard's "The Katherine Peare tree"

BEECH *(Fagus* spp) Tree
Foliage: from mid-June

Of the many kinds of *Plant It Now, Dry It Later* foliage, I find the leaves of the Beech to be the most versatile for use in the dried bouquet. Depending on the species or variety, they may be green, purple, copper-colored, or copper-colored edged in pink and white.

If you have lawn space for a truly great tree, try one of the handsome Beeches: the fern-leaf *asplenifolia;* the Green or Purple Weeping Beech, *pendula,* or *pendula purpurea;* or the magnificent *tricolor* with its three-colored leaves, all of which are varieties of the European Beech, *Fagus sylvatica.* Although it is used for tool handles and inexpensive furniture, Beech wood is short-grained and not particularly durable. Well-ripened Beech nuts produce an oil which is still used for cooking in some European countries.

The American Beech, *Fagus grandifolia,* a forest tree of the eastern United States, has handsome light green, sharply toothed leaves.

To Dry: Beech leaves are processed in glycerin and water as directed on page 90.

Beech

OREGON HOLLY-GRAPE *(Mahonia aquifolium)*
Evergreen shrub

Foliage

The dark green leaves of Oregon Holly-Grape are large, stiff, spiny and lustrous—resembling somewhat the leaves of the English Holly.

About forty-five kinds of *Mahonia* are native to North and Central America and to the east coast of Asia, but only *Mahonia aquifolium* is hardy as far north as my garden.

The plant grows to about three feet in height and in the spring is adorned with clusters of lovely yellow flowers.

Bernard M'Mahon, after whom this shrub was named, was a nineteenth-century American horticulturist.

To Dry: Process the foliage in glycerin and water, page 90.

VERBENA *(Verbena* spp) Annual in my garden;
Perennial in the South

Most of the more than eighty members of the *Verbena* family live in the West, especially in the warmer latitudes. The plants bloom prolifically throughout the entire growing season, producing cluster after cluster of flowers in luscious shades of purple to lavender and blue, red to pink, white, and, occasionally, yellow, on stems up to a foot tall. Verbena is easily grown from seed and is undemanding as to soil conditions. Its ability to withstand drought makes it a good candidate for window-box planting and as a peripheral plant in pot gardens. I often use Verbena to edge the annual beds, and its spreading habit of growth makes it an ideal plant to use as a ground cover among the spikey Lilies and Gladioli.

To Dry: Cut the stem an inch or two below the flower head. Verbena is one of the several clustered flowers that are wired and processed as if they were single flowers. See directions on page 81. Allow three days for processing. Verbena colors dry true with a few exceptions: the pale lavender becomes a beautiful pale blue while the deep reds darken unattractively.

BACHELOR'S BUTTON *(Centaurea cyanus)* Annual

Bachelor's Button, a native of Southeast Europe, is an old-fashioned flower that has never lost its popularity. It is the Bluet in the French garden and was the Blew Bottle, or Corne Floure, in John Gerard's garden, and he describes the plant as follows:

> The common Corne-floure hath leaves spread upon the ground, of a whitish greene colour, somewhat hackt or cut in the edges like those of Corne Scabious; among which riseth up a stalk divided into divers small branches, whereon do grow long leaves of an over-worne greene colour, with few cuts or none at all. The floures grow at the top of the stalkes, of a blew colour, consisting of many small floures set in a sealy or chaffie head like those of the Knapweeds: the seed is smooth, bright shining, and wrapped in a woolly or stocky matter. The root is small and single, and perisheth when it hath perfected his seed.

Gerard also noted that the Bottle flowered in other colors: purple, white, and violet, all of which are available to the home gardener today. Subsequently, horticulturists added another color which was unknown to Gerard: pink.

The plants, which are one foot to two feet tall at maturity, germinate quickly from seed and once sown in the garden are likely to reappear year after year as a result of self-seeding. Bachelor's Buttons are available from the florist throughout most of the year.

To Dry: Bachelor's Buttons should be processed soon after picking as the flowers lose their color during the drying process if the stems are left standing in water for more than a day before processing. Wire and dry as for the single flower, page 81. Allow three days.

SNAPDRAGON (Antirrhinum majus) Tender Perennial (But I grow it as an annual in my garden)

This native of southern Europe and Asia Minor was given its Greek name by someone who fancied that the flower resembled a dragon's snout. The eyes of the Japanese saw a different form, and their old name for this garden favorite meant *golden fish flower.*

Gerard found little of medicinal value in the plant. "The seed of snapdragon is good for nothing in the use of physicke," he wrote, but Dioscorides, 1500 years before, reported "that the herbe being hanged about one preserveth a man from being bewitched and that it maketh a man gracious in the sight of people."

Our garden Snapdragons have been developed from just one of the thirty to forty members of the family: *Antirrhinum majus.* Although the plant survives my northern New Jersey winter if covered with a mulch, I grow it most often as an annual. A light soil, enriched with bone meal and peat moss, will allow for the growth of a sturdy root structure which is important to the plant's stability when the top-heavy, two-and-a-half-foot flower spikes are in bloom. The flowers cover almost every hue of the spectrum but skip the blue. I prefer the Butterfly and Bellflower varieties for drying because of the ease in filling the individual flowers with silica gel when drying.

To Dry: Either a single flower or an entire spray cluster may be dried. Process the single flower as for the single flower, page 81. Allow three days. Process the entire spray cluster as for stalks of flowers, page 86. Allow five days.

CANTERBURY BELLS (Campanula medium) Biennial

Flowers: June and early July

There are many members in the *Campanula* family, but the one that most of us know best is *Campanula medium,* the familiar Canterbury Bells. Its name comes from the Latin *campana,* which means *bell* and so describes the shape of the rose, blue, or white blooms that are formed along the two- to two-and-a-half-foot stems in June and early July in my garden.

Campanula grows well in pots and Elizabeth Kent reported in her *Flora Domestica* on the novel use of the Chimney Plant or Pyramidal Bellflower *(Campanula pyramidalis),* which I suspect will dry as well as the Canterbury Bells:

There is a species of *Campanula* which is trained to conceal fire-places in the summer, and has a very pretty effect when so used. It is the Pyramidal Campanula; *la Pyramidale des Jardins* of the French. The roots send out three or four strong upright stalks, which grow nearly four feet high, and are garnished with smooth oblong leaves and an abundance of large blue flowers. These upright stalks send out short side-branches, which are also adorned with flowers; so that, by spreading the upright stalks to a flat frame composed of slender laths, the whole plant is formed into the shape of a fan, and will perfectly screen a common sized fire-place. The plant may stand abroad till the flowers begin to open, and, being then placed in a room where it is shaded from the sun and rain, the flowers will continue long in beauty. If it be removed into the air at night, where it is not exposed to heavy rains, the flowers will be handsomer, and will last longer. This kind is rather more delicate than those before mentioned; and when raised from seeds, which is the best mode, requires a hot-bed to bring it forward. It should therefore be procured in a pot, and should be one that has been raised from seed. Most of the Campanulas close their flowers at night. They will grow in common garden earth.

To Dry: I prefer to wire and dry these flowers singly, reassembling them later as sprays if that is the way they are to be used in the bouquet. Process according to the directions for flowers that are cuplike in form, page 86, allowing three days for processing.

BABY'S-BREATH (*Gypsophila* spp)

Annual and perennial

Flowers: June through August

Baby's-Breath lends its misty-white beauty to the garden and is unsurpassed as a "filler" for the dried bouquet.

Gypsophila belongs to the Stitchwort family of plants, but of the almost sixty members of the family only a few are worth bothering to grow. The annual Baby's-Breath, *Gypsophila elegans*, is native to the Caucasus. The flowers, either pure white or rosy-pink, are larger than those of their perennial relative, but they grow on shorter stems. They are popular as a filler for fresh flower bouquets.

Gypsophila paniculata, a perennial with tiny white flowers, is an old favorite. New varieties of this species, Bristol Fairy, Pink Fairy, and Perfect, have double white or pink flowers. They are showier in the garden and in the dried bouquet. The plants grow to two and a half to three feet tall and have scant foliage. The stems branch out into many fine, stiff stems which end in small flowers, creating a crown of airy profusion in the garden. To maintain this crown effect and to prevent the flower heads from sagging to the ground I put five bamboo stakes in a one-foot diameter circle around the root in the spring, allowing the stakes to rise about 2 foot and a half above the ground. A string or the paper-covered wire "twist-'ems" is run around the stakes near the top, and this becomes a supporting perimeter for the plant as it grows. Not only does the Baby's-Breath present a neater appearance in the garden, but the support keeps the flower heads from being beaten to the ground and ruined by a heavy rain.

Perennial Baby's-Breath is available from the florist, fresh, through most of the year, and dried in the fall.

To Dry: The clustered head of the annual Baby's-Breath is wired and dried in silica gel as for the single flower, page 96. Allow four days. Cut and hang the perennial Baby's-Breath to allow the stems to harden.

STOCK *(Matthiola incana)* Annual and Biennial
Flowers: Summer and fall, depending on the kind

An old-fashioned favorite, Stock is one of the most sweetly perfumed of all garden flowers. It is a native plant of Europe, Australia, and South Africa, and its botanical name, *Matthiola,* honors the sixteenth-century Italian physician, Peter Andrew Matthioli.

The flowers, in feminine shades of pink, rose, and lavender (plus white and pale yellow), are clustered along sturdy stalks that grow from a dwarfish twelve inches to a tall thirty inches, depending on the variety. The "seven-week" and "ten-week" Stocks are the annual kinds *(Matthiola incana* var. *annua),* and the Brompton Stocks are the biennials.

"Of Stocke Gillofloures," Gerard wrote, "they are not used in Physicke, except amongst certaine Empericks and Quacksalvers, about love and lust matters, which for modestie I omit." Can it be that Gerard is blushing?

To Dry: Process as for sprays of flowers, page 86. Allow five days for all parts to harden.

Gerard's "Stocke Gillofloures"

COCKSCOMB *(Celosia* spp) Annual in my garden; Perennial in the South

Celosia is of two kinds: crested *(Celosia cristata)* and plumed *(Celosia*

Crested Celosia

Plumed Celosia

argentea). Both are *Plant It Now, Dry It Later* favorites that prefer sun and are easy to grow. They have the double attraction of long beauty in the garden and in the dried bouquet. These same flowers were favorites in John Gerard's seventeenth-century garden. He classified them generally as *Amaranthus;* today we call them Everlastings.

Cockscomb, as the crested *Celosia* is most commonly known to American gardeners, derives its name from its resemblance to that barnyard fowl's comb. In Gerard's time the popular name was more poetic: "Velvet floure gentle." Although it is most frequently seen in a barnyard red, Cockscomb is also available in beautiful jewel colors which range from pale yellow to apricot, and from pale and shocking pinks to ruby tones.

The stocky round stem becomes flat and fibrous at the crest, or "ruffle." If the comb is small in size the ruffle is usually continuous. If it is a large comb, it takes on many convolutions which may be several ruffles plus numerous small individual combs on the sides.

To Dry: Cut the stalk near the base and remove the foliage. The large comb is rarely used as a whole in flower arranging and it is easier to divide the stalk when it is freshly cut and still soft. Remove the side combs and pierce each one near the end with a length of wire. Bend the wire about one inch back along its own length, twist, and hang to dry. The stalk can then be divided easily along its fibrous threads and hung with the side combs. If the Cockscomb is cut late in the season and is a variety which you have enjoyed, place a box beneath the drying combs to catch the seeds which fall from beneath the ruffle, to plant in next year's garden.

PLUMED CELOSIA

Gerard's popular name for the plumed *Celosia* in his garden was "Purple-floure gentle." The name in itself attests to the work of horticulturists in the last three centuries for to Gerard's purple color has been added gold. Occasionally you may find an anomaly, as I did one year when one plant developed an almost white plume. Besides the single large plume, the plant produces small shoots from its single stalk which are very useful in smaller arrangements.

To Dry: Cut the stalk near the ground; remove the foliage and hang to dry. The dried plume will look rather stiff and lusterless, but its soft appearance and sheen can be restored quickly by rotating the plume over steam from the kettle for a few minutes.

STATICE (Limonium)

There are two species of *Limonium* that are useful to the dried bouquet, and they are both commonly called Statice. Inasmuch as they are quite different in appearance considerable confusion often arises between buyer and seller (whether of plants, seeds, or cut flowers) when the buyer has one species in mind and the seller, the other. The following, it is hoped, will clarify the distinction between the two.

Gerard's "Limonium," or "Sea Lavender"

SEA LAVENDER (Limonium latifolium)   Perennial
Flowers: Late August

This plant grows along the shore from Maine to Florida as well as many other places in the world, and it is available in either plant or seed to the home gardener. I use it as I do Baby's-Breath—as an airy filler in the dried bouquet. The following is Gerard's description of the plant from his *Herball*, and if you will persist with his "olde English" you should find it as informative as I did. The plant "has faire leaves, like the Limon or Orenge tree, but of a dark green color, somewhat fatter and a little crumpled, among which leaves riseth up an hard and brittle naked stalk of a foot high, divided at the top into sundry other small branches, which grow for the most part upon the one side, full of little bluish flowers, in shew like Lavender, with long red seed, and a thicke root like unto the small dock."

To Dry: Cut the stems when the tiny flowers are in full bloom and hang until ready to use. In New Jersey I associate its cutting with Labor Day. It is available, dried, from the local florist in September and October.

STATICE (Limonium sinuatum)
                Annual in New Jersey; Biennial further south
This plant has none of the airy appearance of the Sea Lavender. The flower heads are more tightly clustered, and the colors, which range from white to pale and hot pinks, blues, and lavenders, are a far cry from the "blew" color mentioned by Gerard; but his plant description is excellent:

From a long, slender root comes forth long green leaves lying spread upon the ground, being deeply sinuated (wavy) on both sides, and somewhat roughish. Amongst these leaves grow up stalks welted

Statice

with slender indented skinnes, and toward their tops they are divided into sundry branches after the manner of the ordinary one, but these branches are also winged and at their tops they carry flowers some four or five clustering together, consisting of one thin crispe or crumpled leaf of a light blew colour (which continues long if you gather them in their perfect vigor, and so dry them) and in the middle of this blew comes up little white flowers. This plant was first observed by Rauwolf at Joppa in Syria, but it also grows on the coasts of Barbarie, and at Malacca and Cadiz in Spaine.

Limonium sinuatum requires full sun and is easy to grow from seed. It does not transplant well, however, so the seed should be sown where the plants are to grow.

To Dry: Gather them, as Gerard says, "in their perfect vigor," that is, when the tiny white flowers begin to appear. Bundle about six stems together and hang to dry. The colorful bracts are everlasting in texture and are already dry, but the stems are soft and must be given time to dry and harden. This takes about two weeks. It is available from the florist in abundance February through April; and in lesser quantity in the fall.

ZINNIA *(Zinnia elegans)* Annual

This colorful flower, which has its home in Mexico, gained its name from Johann Gottfied Zinn (1727–1759), who was Professor of Botany at Gottingen.

Zinnias provide vibrant color in the sunny garden and many a bright spot in the dried bouquet. Propagation is by seed, so consult the seedsmen's catalogs for the many varieties available. For drying, choose the flatter-petaled, rather than the curled-petaled, varieties. All colors dry well in silica gel with the exception of vermillion and deep red, which darken considerably. Zinnias are not self-branching before flowering, so the top inch should be nipped off when the plants are five to six inches tall to encourage branching, which, in turn, produces more flowers.

To Dry: Process as for the single flower, page 81, wiring as suggested in either section two or three. Allow two to two and a half days for drying.

Zinnia stems dry well and may be used in arranging. After cutting off the flower head simply remove the foliage and stand the stem in a glass to dry.

DEVILWOOD *(Osmanthus americanus)* Shrub

Foliage: From August 1

This evergreen shrub is not usually recommended in a latitude as far north as my garden, although my hedge has survived very well. It is more common in Virginia, and many of our federal buildings in Washington are graced with the shiny, evergreen, Holly-like leaves of these beautiful plants. In spite of the similarity of the leaves, Devilwood is not related to the Holly, and the easiest way to distinguish the two is by observing where the leaves appear along the stem: A pair of Devilwood leaves appear directly opposite each other, while Holly leaves occur alternately.

Small potted plants of Devilwood, looped with artificial red berries, are often sold at Christmas time as "Holly."

To Dry: Cut when the new growth has hardened, usually about August 1. Process in glycerin and water as directed on page 90.

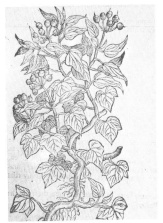

Gerard's "Clymbing or berried Ivy," and

IVY *(Hedera helix)* Creeping Shrub

Foliage

"There be two kinds of Ivy reckoned among the number of those plants which have need to be propped up, for they stand not of themselves but are fastened to stone walls, trees and such like," said Gerard. One is a "climbing Ivy that lifteth herselfe to the tops of trees, the other Ivy creepeth upon the ground."

Gerard was uncertain as to how to categorize the Ivy. He thought they were "not to be placed among the trees, shrubs, or bushes, because of the affinitie they have with climbing herbes; as also agreeing in forme and figure with many other plants that climbe, and are indeed simply to be reckoned among the herbes that clamber up."

The uses of Ivy in our gardens today are much the same as they were in Gerard's garden, although I suspect a greater variety is available to us than was available to him.

To Dry: Sprays of Ivy may be processed in glycerin and water, page 90; single leaves in silica gel, page 93.

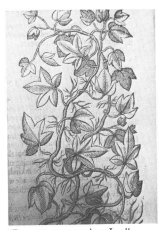

"Barren or creeping Ivy"

AMERICAN HOLLY *(Ilex opaca)* Tree

Foliage

Who needs a Christmas Tree when there is a red-berried Holly just outside the door? The American Holly, *Ilex opaca,* is my favorite ornamental evergreen tree, and is a native plant in New Jersey. Actually, it is native to a much larger area that extends from Massachusetts to Florida, and westward to Texas.

There are male and female Hollies, but only the female has the berries. The male is not dispensable, however, and one must be nearby to pollinate the female flowers in June if she is to bear her gorgeous red berries in the fall.

The tree resembles a cone and sometimes attains a height of fifty feet. Holly should be transplanted either in the early fall when the new wood has hardened, or in the early spring before the new growth appears. When growing Holly from the berries, care must be taken to leave them undisturbed as two years are required for germination.

To Dry: Cut the branches from August 1, and process in glycerin and water as directed on page 90.

JUNIPER (Juniperus communis var. *depressa)* Shrub
Foliage

Gerard's "small Juniper of the Alps"

Juniper is native only in the northern hemisphere. There are about forty members of the family—some, like Red Cedar, are tall trees, others are short shrubs—some grow only in the south, others grow only in the north. Common Juniper *(Juniperus communis)* is a tree or shrub that grows to forty feet, but the variety which is included here, *depressa*, means, as you might guess, that its height has been depressed, and these spreading shrubs rarely exceed four feet. They are often grown as a ground cover for broad open areas.

In Gerard's day the berries, with "oile of lineseed, mixed together" made "a liquor called vernish, which is used to beautifie pictures and painted tables with, and to make iron glisten, and to defend it from rust."

Their medicinal use in the seventeenth century was to "clense the liver and kidnies; being over largely taken it causeth gripings and gnawings in the stomach and maketh the head hot; it provoketh urine."

Today, Juniper berries are used to flavor gin.

To Dry: Process in glycerin and water, page 90.

STRAWFLOWER (Helichrysum bracteatum) Annual

There seem to be more kinds of Everlastings on the land mass of Australia than in most other parts of the world, and the Strawflower has been the most popular Everlasting ever to migrate to our American gardens from that down-under continent. *Helichrysum* is Greek and means *sun* and *gold*, which tells us not only where the plant should be grown but also the original color of the flower. Today, thanks to the efforts of horticulturists, large double flowers in shades of pink, yellow, mustard gold, red, and white appear on the sturdy two-and-a-half- to three-foot-tall stems, and are known as *Helichrysum monstrosum.*

Strawflowers have become an important commercial flower in the United States, and they bloom in great profusion at the local florist's in the fall and in lesser numbers during the year.

To Dry: These Lazy Flowers appear sequentially on the plant and the maximum number of flowers can be gathered during the growing season if they are picked singly. See page 71.

MARIGOLD (*Tagetes* spp)   Annual

The Marigold is spectacularly showy in the garden and is among the most satisfactory of dried flowers. It retains a particularly fresh appearance when processed in silica gel and is less susceptible to higher summer humidity than most of the other More Effort Flowers. Lost in the drying process, and not unhappily, is the pungent aroma of the stem and foliage. Most of our large garden Marigolds are the progeny of the single-flowered African Marigold *(Tagetes erecta)*, and hybridizers have developed a wide range of colors from almost white through yellow, gold, and orange. An exception is the Burpee Nugget which has a partial ancestry in the French Marigold *(Tagetes patula)*. I sometimes use these fast-germinating, foot-tall beauties to edge the annual bed, for they assure me large flowers and continuous bloom throughout the growing season. I avoid drying the small, red-centered French Marigolds because of the unattractive color change which they undergo during the drying process.

Marigold

To Dry: Wire and dry as for the single flower, page 81. Allow four days for small flowers, seven days for the large blooms.

When dry, the hollow stems of the Marigold may be used as stems for dried flowers to give a natural appearance to the dried bouquet. Simply cut the stems, strip them of their foliage, and stand in a jar or vase to allow them to dry and harden.

CHENILLE PLANT (*Acalypha hispida*)
RED-HOT CATTAIL PLANT
Tender Shrub—but grown as an annual in my garden

Flowers: Summer and fall in my garden

This native of Burma accommodates itself in a modest way to northern New Jersey's climate. In the winter it survives only as a house or greenhouse plant, but during the summer it is interesting in a hanging basket or grown as a pot garden plant.

The one-and-a-half-foot-long flower spikes resemble cats' tails; they are bright red in color and chenillelike in texture which account for its two popular names. A variety, *alba,* has white tails. The flowers have an everlasting quality similar to that of plumed Celosia and Gerard thought that the two plants belonged to the same family. He called this one *Amaranthus pannicula sparsa,* or *Branched Floure-Gentle.* He said of it: "This is seldom to be found with us; but for the beauties sake is kept in the Gardens of Italy, whereas the women esteemed it not only for the comliness and beautious aspect, but also for the efficacy thereof against the bloody issues, and sanious ulcers of the wombe and kidneys."

Freshly cut branches are available in limited quantity from the florist in the fall.

To Dry: Cut and hang to allow the stems to harden.

REED GRASS *(Phragmites communis)* Perennial
Flowers: In the summer

Reed Grass

The giant Reed Grass is to be found in open, moist areas in almost all parts of the United States and southern Canada, as well as along the Mediterranean Sea, and in the Middle East. It proliferates in the meadows of northern New Jersey where it covers thousands of acres west of the Hudson River. In late July the silky, sable-toned, feathery flowers begin to rise above the grass to reach heights up to fifteen feet. As summer progresses these flowers become a great sea of plumes, bending and swaying as the winds sweep over the meadows.

The plant has had little usefulness for us in the western hemisphere, but it has served the people of the Mediterranean much as bamboo has served the people of the Far East. It has provided many a fishing pole, and many a pipe, both the smoking kind and the kind that Pan played, and when woven it has enclosed and protected many a vegetable garden.

Like bamboo, the stems of the Reed Grass are hollow, and I use them to add extra length to the short stems of Bittersweet and other stiff-stemmed materials. Incidentally, Red Grass and Bittersweet, arranged together, are handsome on the autumn hearth.

To Dry: Cut the stems while the flowers are in the silky, feathery stage which is until late August. Some will retain their silky appearance but most will mature to become fluffy plumes. If cut very much later than early September, the flower heads tend to deteriorate, sending bits of fluff circulating with each disturbance of the surrounding air. Reed Grass requires no processing. Simply cut and stand in an umbrella stand or similar deep container until needed.

There are three genera of wild Everlasting plants in the United States that are so similar in appearance that they are often thought to belong to the same genus. Their popular names are often used interchangeably, which is understandable because their pearly-white or grayish-white everlasting flowers bear such a strong resemblance to each other. They all grow in dry, open places, and all attain maximum heights of three feet. The flower dryer will not be too concerned about the differences between these plants except to note their flowering times and where they grow; but to sort them out botanically:

EVERLASTINGS IN EVERYONE'S ROADSIDE GARDEN: PICK WITH CARE!

PEARLY EVERLASTING (Anaphalis margaritacea)
Perennial

Flowers: July through September

Pearly Everlasting has the whitest flowers of the three plants and perhaps the most desirable for the dried bouquet. It is now available from reliable nurserymen for the home garden under its botanical name, *Anaphalis.* In its wild state it is found in a latitude ranging from Newfoundland to New York, but it crops up in other places, such as New Mexico and in the higher altitudes of North Carolina. The plant is also well known in Asia and Europe.

PUSSY-TOES, LADIES' TOBACCO (Antennaria sp)
Perennial

Flowers: April to June

Pussy-Toes resemble minute, clustered Strawflowers. They are somewhat more gray in color than the Pearly Everlasting. The plant is found growing from Maine to Georgia, and at least as far west as the Missouri River.

CUDWEED, CATFOOT (Gnaphalium sp) Perennial

Flowers: August to November

This plant spans the continent from the east to the west coast, and from southern Canada to Florida. The grayish color of the flowers seems less dingy if the stems are picked before the tubular flower heads have fully opened. The plant is "wooly" and as the flowers dry fluffs of wool appear from what seems to be nowhere. Before using this flower in an arrangement, I usually take the bunches outdoors for a final shake to remove any remaining "wool."

To Dry: All three everlastings are cut and hung to dry. Hanging the stems in a paper bag will help to contain the fluffs of wool of the Cudweed.

HOLLYHOCK *(Althaea rosea)*
Perennial, but best grown as a biennial
Flowers: From early June through mid-summer

The Hollyhock has been grown in Europe since the Crusaders carried the seed from the Holy Land where the plant had paused in its westward migration from China. In the Middle East *hoc* means *mallow,* and it is presumed that the Crusaders named it "Holy Hoc," which has since degenerated to its present popular name.

The Hollyhock was a favorite in old-fashioned gardens, and the resurgence of its popularity is due, in part, to the beautiful double varieties, such as the Pompadour, which have been developed. Although the Hollyhock is a perennial, it is reliable only when grown as a biennial. It is one of our taller plants and belongs at the back of the sunny border where its stiff, vertical line of blossoms adds interest to the garden.

To Dry: Because of its extremely short stem the flower must be processed as soon as it is picked. Wire, and dry the single kinds as for flowers that are cuplike in form, page 86; the double kinds as for the single flower, page 81. Allow three days for processing. The Mallows, Hollyhock, and Rose of Sharon, are among the flowers whose forms are most susceptible to change when exposed to high summer humidity. See "Storing Your Dried Materials," page 97.

CHRYSANTHEMUM *(Chrysanthemum* spp) Perennial
Flowers: Late summer through the fall

Some *Plant It Now, Dry It Later* members of the Chrysanthemum family such as Shasta Daisy, Feverfew, Ox-Eye Daisy, and the Painted Daisy that bloom in the late spring and early summer are so widely known by their popular names that, for convenience, I have listed them separately. The autumn-flowering members of the family seem not to have acquired popular names in English and continue to be known by their botanical name, or simply as Mums.

The Chrysanthemum has been called "the flower of the East, as the Rose is the flower of the West," and there seem to be as many legends and stories told of one as of the other. The plant is a native of China and festivals and celebrations in honor of the Chrysanthemum have been held in that country since ancient times. Medicinally, the flower was a virtual fountain of youth if the restorative powers attributed to it are to be believed: A drink of morning dew collected from the flowers would restore health and vitality; to drink the waters of a pool beside which Chrysanthemums grew would assure an age of at least one hundred years. Petals of this flower are still widely used in the Chinese diet, and they are interesting and colorful additives to our American salad bowl.

The Chrysanthemum seems to have arrived in Holland from East Asia in 1688, but it died there either from lack of knowledge of (or interest in) its cultivation. One hundred years later it was introduced into France where its cultivation was successful.

The gardener has a wide variety of Chrysanthemums from which to choose. All are magnificent in the garden but not all retain their form through the drying process. When planning a garden with the intention of drying some Chrysanthemums, do grow the twelve-inch Cushion Mums in garden borders and the taller Button Mums such as "Little One" to stand behind, and the large-flowered varieties such as "Charles Nye" to occupy the taller garden places. Avoid the Spoon and Cactus-Petaled kinds as well as others whose petals are markedly convex.

To Dry: Wire and process as for the single flower, page 81. Allow four days for the Button Mums, seven days for the other kinds. Yellows, whites, and pinks dry well but some shades of red and orange are disappointing.

CORN, ORNAMENTAL (*Zea mays* var. *japonica*)
Annual

Corn in the flower bed? Certainly, if you are planting the colorful ornamental Corn for its decorative value—and not in the formal bed, of course!

In my own garden I plan for a dozen stalks and plant the kernels, three to a hole, to the back of the sunny border. They provide an interesting background in that part of the garden and seldom fail to evoke a surprised "*Corn* in your flower bed?" The full-sized variegated ears are useful in the larger, free-standing arrangements, while the ornamental two-inch mahogany-red ears of the Strawberry Popcorn lend themselves well to table and wall decorations.

Ornamental Corn

To Dry: Depending on the variety, Ornamental Corn is ready for harvest in 105–110 days from planting.

Cut the stalk near the ground and again, carefully, about two inches above the ear. Gently draw the husk from the ear but *do not remove.* Do remove the silk from the kernels. The effect should be that of a flower—the husk resembling the petals and the ear resembling the flower center.

Crumpled paper toweling tucked into the husk and held in place with a few straight pins will retard shrinkage of the husk during drying. Round off the husk tips with scissors.

As the parts of the Corn dry they shrink, and I sometimes secure the ear to the stalk with wire as described in "Repairs and Reinforcements," page 114.

CHINESE LANTERN   *(Physalis alkekengi)*
Perennial

Fruits: Fall

Chinese Lanterns have been known to, and grown by, gardeners for so many centuries that no one is quite sure when the plant first began its westward migration from Eastern Asia. We do know that it was well known in Europe in the fifteenth century, and it is readily identified among the flowers so beautifully woven into the medieval Unicorn Tapestries which hang at the Cloisters in New York City. Its botanical name, *Physalis*, is from the Greek *physa* which means *bladder*, an appropriate term for the inflated red-orange lantern fruit. It is also popularly known as Winter Cherry and Cape Gooseberry.

Plant the seed in a sunny spot in the garden, but do not expect the lanterns until the second year. Except for the newer dwarf varieties, the plants grow to about two feet in height. They require little attention and spread very freely.

To Dry: Cut the stems in the fall when the fruit is formed and its color is bright. Hang them in small bunches adjusting the angle of hanging to allow the lanterns to retain their natural, pendulous appearance as they dry.

SUNFLOWER   *(Helianthus annuus)*
Annual: Cultivated or Wild

Flowers: July to November

Among the most common of the yellow wildflowers that cast their golden glow in meadows and along the roadside in summer and fall are the Sunflowers. There are more than thirty members of the Sunflower family growing wild in the United States, and they vary in height from one foot to fifteen feet. This particular Sunflower *(Helianthus annuus)* reaches these maximum heights in the meadows of northern New Jersey as it competes with the giant Reed Grass for the rays of the sun. Although prolific in its growth, consideration must be given to its survival. Each year I must go deeper into the meadows to pick these beauties as they retreat before the advance of industry. Should you prefer to cultivate this or another annual, or one of the perennial Sunflowers such as *Helianthus decapetalus* or *Helianthus tuberosus* in your garden, seeds and plants are readily available from seedmen and nurserymen under their botanical name Helianthus. The cultivated "birdseed" Sunflower is *Helianthus annuus* var. *macrosperma.* This one I do not attempt to dry but, rather, leave it for the birds!

Sunflowers

To Dry: Most Sunflowers should dry well, but the flowers must be picked and dried before they are too mature or you may find yourself gluing the petals back in place after processing—not a difficult task but an unnecessary one if consideration is given to timing, page 79. Wire and dry as for the single flower, page 81. The petals are dry in three days but allow four days for processing to permit the calyxlike green phyllaries to dry.

LILY-OF-THE-VALLEY TREE *(Oxydendron arboreum)*
Tree

SOURWOOD TREE

Foliage

There is just one member in the *Oxydendron* family and it lives in eastern North America. It is a small- to medium-sized ornamental tree of easy culture that is ideal when planted as a specimen for the small lawn. It produces white flowers in the summer that look remarkably like the spring-flowering Lily-of-the-Valley, hence one of its popular names. The other, Sourwood, is a reflection on the flavor of the oblong leaves that are bright green in summer, turning scarlet in the fall. It is for its foliage rather than its flower that this tree is of importance to the *Plant It Now, Dry It Later* gardener.

To Dry: Process in glycerin and water as directed on page 90. The green leaves turn a tawny gold but the scarlet foliage remains true to color.

PIN OAK *(Quercus palustris)* Tree
Foliage

The use to which I put the mighty Oak seems humble indeed when one compares it to the ships its wood has built, the leather its bark has tanned, and the hogs its acorns have fed. Of the more than 200 species of Oak that grow in the cooler regions of the northern hemisphere, it is the deciduous Pin Oak, *Quercus palustris,* that grows in my garden. This handsome tree, whose green summer leaves turn to shades of red in autumn, is a native of the area cornered by Massachusetts, Delaware, Arkansas, and Wisconsin. Its foliage, and very likely the foliage of other Oaks, may be processed for use in the dried bouquet.

To Dry: Process in glycerin and water as directed on page 90.

DAHLIA *(Dahlia* spp) Annual in my garden
Perennial (Tuberous) further south

Dwarf single-bedding Dahlia

Dahlias come in many sizes, but for use in the small dried bouquet I prefer the dwarf varieties. They lend themselves well to sunny beddings and borders in the garden where they flower profusely through summer and autumn until frost. My favorites are the pompoms and the dwarf single-bedding Dahlias, particularly the Siemon Doorents and the red Wiek which is prolific in its flowering, and sensational as a border plant. The red of the Wiek darkens slightly in processing but is still very pretty.

Come October, Dahlias flaunt their showy heads from the centers of the *corbeille de fleurs* or formal flower beds in the Jardin des Plantes in Paris. These particularly eye-catching plants are three to four feet tall, and many of their flowers appear to be big brothers to our more familiar single-bedding Dahlias. They include such beauties as the white "Sirene" with its orange center, and the yellow "Source d'Or." Double or multi-petaled varieties are the pink "Symbol" and the yellow "Yellow Jewel." These are all *Plant It Now, Dry It Later* flowers that are a bonus in the garden and in the larger dried bouquet. They are colorful and well proportioned for the sunny border, and an increase in their availability should be met with great enthusiasm by the American home gardener.

Europeans discovered the Dahlia in Mexico at the time of the Spanish Conquest where Aztec horticulturists already had developed varieties different from the native wild plant. Linnaeus gave this Central American beauty the name Dahlia, thereby honoring his pupil, Swedish Botanist Andreas Dahl.

Dahlias may be started from seed or grown from tubers. Earlier flowering will be achieved by starting the seed indoors six to eight weeks before outdoor planting is anticipated. If you like the variety you have grown, dig the tubers after the first frost and store them for division and planting in next year's garden.

To Dry: Wire and dry as for the single flower, page 81. Allow three to four days for processing.

ROSE OF SHARON *(Hibiscus syriacus)*

Shrub, deciduous

Flowers: From midsummer depending on variety

Rose of Sharon has been a favorite in European gardens since its arrival from Turkey centuries ago. The shrub grows to a height of ten to twelve feet and is often grown as an informal, colorful hedge. Pruning increases the size of the flowers and in small French gardens, where single specimens are often pruned to a size and form resembling a rose-tree, the flowers are enormous.

The Mallow-type flowers are sequential in their flowering along the branches and are of short duration, which makes them difficult to use in fresh flower arrangements; but their shades of pink, white, and blue, when dried, will add a new quality and interest to your dried bouquet.

To Dry: Rose of Sharon is short-stemmed like the Hollyhock and must be processed immediately after picking. Wire and dry as for flowers that are cuplike in form, page 86.

PINCUSHION FLOWER *(Scabiosa* spp)
BLUE BONNET
WHITE BONNET

Annual or Perennial

Flowers: The annuals from July until frost; The perennials from June to September

Gerard's "Common Scabious"

Scabiosa is the old Latin word for *itch,* and, referring to its medicinal virtues, Gerard wrote "It is reported that it cureth scabs, if the decoction thereof be drunke certain daies, and the juice used in ointments." Unfortunately Gerard does not tell us *which* days! It also "scoureth the chest and lungs; it is good against an old cold, shortness of breath, pain in the sides, and such like infirmities of the chest." A real cure-all!

The stamens of the cultivated annual *Scabiosa (Scabiosa atropurpurea)* resemble pins stuck into a cushion—hence one of its popular names. Blue Bonnet and White Bonnet are the common names applied to the perennial *Scabiosa (Scabiosa caucasica),* and they indicate not only the color of the flower but something of its shape. The flowers of the annual plants range from white to pink through the lavenders to a dark mahogany-red.

The long flower stems (two feet to three feet) of these sun-loving natives of Europe, Africa, and Asia have made *Scabiosa* a favorite for fresh flower cutting both in gardens at home and in the gardens of America.

To Dry: Wire and dry as for the single flower, page 81. Allow three days. Only the mahogany-red color seems to undergo a change in color during processing, and this darkens unattractively. All other colors remain true.

HARDY AGERATUM　(Eupatorium coelestinum)
HEMP AGRIMONY
MISTFLOWER

Perennial

Flowers: August until frost

Hardy Ageratum

Hardy Ageratum *(Eupatorium coelestinum)* is a common field and roadside plant, found in the area south of a line drawn from New Jersey to Michigan, that is now cultivated in our gardens. Its flossy lavender flowers resemble the annual Ageratum, although they are not quite so large.

Hardy Ageratum does well in sun or light shade. The lavender flowers, atop their foot to foot-and-a-half stems, are outstanding among yellow Chrysanthemums. I also like to plant them in close proximity to Dogwood where the masses of lavender beneath the clusters of red-orange berries create an early autumn sight not soon forgotten.

The popular names of some other species of the genus *Eupatorium,* Boneset and Thoroughwort, attest to the medicinal virtues ascribed to them by the Indians and early settlers. These virtues actually extend to ancient times, however, and the name of this plant family honors Eupator, King of Pontus, who is supposed to have discovered the healing properties of one of its members.

To Dry: Process as for flower clusters on sturdy stems, page 86. Allow three days.

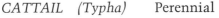

CATTAIL　(Typha)　Perennial
Flowers: late summer

Happy to have its feet wet, the common Cattail *(Typha latifolia)* is found along lakes and streams and in other low permanently wet places where it is a tasty tidbit for muskrats. The Cattail is rampant in its propagation through root running and the species recommended for use in home gardening (*Typha augustifolia,* which attains a height of six feet, and *Typha minima,* which grows to one and a half feet) should be planted only if precautions are taken to contain their roots. This can be done by planting the root in a five-gallon drum from which the bottom has been removed.

To Dry: Cut in August or early September and stand in a tall vase until ready for use. The cutting time is important for if the Cattail is cut too late the minute flowers which form its sleek, smooth surface deteriorate and the "tail" appears to break apart.

IRONWEED *(Vernonia noveborecensis)* Perennial wildflower

Flowers: Mid-July into fall

William Vernon, an English botanist who sought new plants in North America to introduce into European gardens, has lent his name to a very large family of plants. There are well over 500 species of *Vernonia* around the world; in the tropics some of these are shrubs and trees, but I identify this plant, *Vernonia noveborecensis,* as a pretty weed that adds its Thistle-like puffs of purple and rose to the gold of the Goldenrod and the rose of the Aster in the pageant of late summer color along the roadside. Other species are found in the West and South.

To Dry: Ironweed droops quickly when cut but its fresh appearance is quickly restored by cutting an inch from the stems and standing them in water. The processing is the same as that for Thistle, below.

THISTLE *(Cirsium* spp) Biennial wildflower

Flowers: July to mid-August

To the patchwork of summer roadside color the Thistle adds its lavender, and to the winter bouquet this same lavender adds an unexpected and refreshing bit of color.

The Thistle bears flowers in great abundance in the Holy Land at Eastertime. Huge fluffy heads of rose, purple, and white are surrounded by great thorns, and the story told there is that the fluffy-colored heads represent the head of Christ, and the thorns the mock crown placed on his head by the Roman centurions.

Thistle resting on silica gel

To Dry: Cut the stem as the color begins to show. The flower head will continue to open as it dries so the cutting time is important. If cut too late the head will tend to break apart during the processing.

Thistles may be hung to dry but the color takes on a slightly brownish tone. I prefer to process it for 2 days in silica gel, which helps it to retain its lovely, natural color.

GLADIOLUS (*Gladiolus* spp)   Tender corm in my garden, hardy Perennial in the south

Flowers: Summer into fall depending on variety

Most of our beautiful garden varieties of Gladiolus are descendents of hybrids among several members of this large South African family (there are at least 160 wild relatives living in Africa, along the Mediterranean, and in Western Asia). Our name for this herb is derived from the swordlike shape of its leaves (the Latin for sword is *gladius*), while its old Japanese name meant *foreign iris.*

Every year hybridizers introduce new strains of Gladiolus, and those now available to the home gardener cover almost every shade and hue of the spectrum. Hybridization has also varied the blooming times of the bulbs which has extended the blooming season of these gracious spikes of flowers.

The Gladiolus corms do not survive the cold of winter in my garden, so in the fall I dig the new corms which have grown on top of the old ones to save for next year's planting. Often there are tiny cormels clustered against the new corm; these are the offspring of the corm, and they, too, should be stored and planted the following year. They produce flowers in either the first or second year and are the best means of propagating a favorite variety.

To Dry: The flowers dry best when dried singly and may be reassembled to their spikelike form when they are to be arranged. Nip the flower from the stem, wire, and process for flowers that are cuplike in form, page 86. Allow four days for processing.

ASTER (*Callistephus chinensis*)   Annual
CHINA ASTER

Although the names are the same and both are late summer– and fall-flowering plants, this annual Aster, which has its home in China and Siberia, should not be confused with our native perennial Asters. The first seeds of the annual Aster to arrive in Europe were sent from China by a Jesuit Missionary, R. P. d'Incarville, in 1731. It was reported that the seeds produced white-, blue-, and violet-colored single flowers. Seeds of red single flowers and red and blue double flowers gradually arrived in Europe. Today, thanks to the eighteenth-century English botanist Philip Miller, our magnificent Asters cover a wide range of cyanic tones, or those I refer to as the sensuous, feminine shades of blue, red, pink, lavender, and purple. The plants are freely branching and grow to two and a half feet tall, which puts them behind the border planting in the annual bed. Sometimes I use the more recently developed dwarf varieties for edging, which leaves the "loge" in my Theater of Plants for other *Plant It Now, Dry It Later* annuals.

To Dry: Wire, and dry as for the single flower, page 81, allowing five to seven days for processing.

GLOBE AMARANTH *(Gomphrena globosa)*   Annual

Globe Amaranth is one of the most charming flowers for your garden and for the dried bouquet, and it was a favorite of the eighteenth-century Colonial Williamsburg housewife.

At first glance this globular everlasting flower from India is often mistaken for Clover, so similar is it in form to that common wildflower. Globe Amaranth, however, produces a profusion of lovely pink, white, and magenta flowers on bushy, two-foot-tall plants that last through the growing season. Grow them immediately behind the front row of the sunny border. The Greek *amarantos* means *unfading,* and these Clover-like flowers are just that—their colors can be enjoyed for years.

Seedsmen predict about fifteen days for the germination of the seed, but I have found it to vary from eight days, when the planting was followed by unusually hot weather, to almost four weeks during one cold, wet spring. This is to say, of course, that the gardener should not be discouraged if the seedlings do not appear in fifteen days. Gardening sometimes requires a little patience, but the rewards for patience can be very great indeed.

To Dry: The flower stems may be cut and hung to dry from midsummer on. I prefer to leave the plants for summer and autumn color, cutting the plant near the root only when it is threatened by frost. The strawlike flowers are already dry when cut, but the stems are too soft for immediate use. See "How to Dry the Lazy Flowers," page 71. The leaves may be removed either before or after the stems have hardened. Like your other dried materials, the stems of the Globe Amaranth are more brittle when dry, and some care must be taken in handling to avoid breaking them at their lobsterlike joints.

GOLDENROD (*Solidago* spp)
Perennial; Wild or cultivated
Flowers: August through September

> The Sun has shown on the earth
> And the Goldenrod is his fruit.

So wrote Thoreau of this common wildflower that casts a blanket of gold over the countryside in the late summer and early fall. Once erroneously considered to be a source of great distress to allergy sufferers (Ragweed is the demon), Goldenrod is now being cultivated for the garden where it thrives in a dry, sunny situation. In another day this perennial herb was thought to have healing properties, and so its botanical name, *Solidago*, is from the Latin *solido,* which means to make whole.

Goldenrod is a wonderful filler for the dried bouquet where the profusion of tiny fluffs of gold form a bright background for individual flowers of greater importance. Arrange it, too, as the focal point of a bouquet. However you arrange Goldenrod you, like Thoreau, will feel that the sunshine of summer has been stored in its golden sprays.

Goldenrod

To Dry: Goldenrod is one of the very few flowers which do not continue to mature after picking, so it must be cut at the height of its bloom for the best color. If it is cut too early it will remain an unattractive green; if cut too late it will have begun to darken.

There are more kinds of Goldenrod than there are pickles and if you do your harvesting in an open field you will probably find many different plant forms. The golden sprays of one variety may be erect while its neighbor may present a cascading appearance. All forms dry readily in air. For the best effects cater to the natural grace of the plant: bundle and hang the erect varieties; stand those which cascade in tall jars. The appearance of the dried Goldenrod will be enhanced and its color retention improved if it is processed in silica gel for three days. Store all in a dark place until needed to insure the least amount of fading.

TANSY (*Tanacetum vulgare*) Perennial
Flowers: Late July through late August

Not all of the golden glory of late summer belongs to the Goldenrod. Tansy, an herb from eastern Europe that has migrated to the United States, produces its mustard-yellow buttons from late July through late August. It grows particularly well in dry, uncared-for places, and it proliferates between the ties of abandoned railways. The leaves have a strong, pungent aroma that I find unpleasant. In an earlier day, the leaves were used to make a tea taken as a tonic, and which was given to children with

Tansy

measles "to make the measles come out." One friend, who grows it as an herb in his garden, enjoys a fresh leaf or two nightly in his salad.

To Dry: Cut the sturdy stems before the button flowers become too full and convex. If cut too late they take on a brownish tinge, still attractive but not so colorful. Remove foliage and hang to dry.

BITTERSWEET (*Celastrus* spp)   Vine
Fruits: In the fall

Throughout my childhood this trailing, climbing vine with its magnificent clusters of red berries was associated with the brilliance of autumn foliage, great open fireplaces, and crisp, sparkling air tinged with the aroma of cider.

Through the years the popularity of Bittersweet for autumn and winter decoration has lead to indiscriminate picking and in places its consequent near-extinction as a native wild plant. However, home gardeners can preserve this beauty for future generations by planting the cultivated kinds that are now available. Try the *Celastrus scandens,* the giant *Celastrus angulatus,* or the newly introduced *Celastrus loeseneri* from western China.

Except for a sunny or lightly shaded position in the garden, Bittersweet is rather indifferent to its soil and situation. Allow plenty of room for plant growth for this vine usually grows to twenty feet. It is particularly attractive when trained to grow along walls and rustic fences.

To Dry: Cut when the outer orange cover bursts open, exposing the red berries. Bundle and hang until ready to use.

CHINESE CHIVES (*Allium tuberosum*)   Hardy Bulb
Flowers: August–September

How the sweet fragrance of this flower belies its Onion stem! The plants in our American gardens have come, indeed, from all parts of the world. This member of the Onion family is a native of Malabar and was grown in the gardens of Bengal.

As the East India Company's trading vessels sailed the seas between England and the Far East, they stopped at points in between, where they established botanical gardens—"The utility of Botanical Gardens is so universally acknowledged, that there is now scarcely a civilized state in the world which has not one or more of them," wrote W. Carey in the Introduction to *Hortus Bengalensis,* a catalogue of the plants growing in the East India Company's Botanical Garden at Calcutta in 1814. These

Chinese Chives

Gardens became way-stations for plants that were being transported from one part of the globe to another; they often traded plants, not only for their visual beauty but in an effort to establish alien plants of commercial value in a new soil. Chinese Chives, a 1½-foot-tall member of the Onion family took up residence at the Garden in Calcutta shortly before 1814. Like the garden Chive, the leaves of this plant are useful in salads.

To Dry: Dry in a tall container as directed for flower clusters on sturdy stems, page 86. Allow three days. The sweet scent of the flower is lost in the processing but the Onion odor of the stem lives on for about six weeks.

EUCALYPTUS   (Eucalyptus cinerea)   Tree
SILVER DOLLAR TREE
Foliage

The branches of this Eucalyptus grow in the local florist garden in northern New Jersey, but in California they grow on small trees. The foliage is interesting—the stiff, round, silvery leaves look like silver dollars marching in pairs along graceful stems. Another type has stiff, round, reddish-brown leaves. Both retain their color and form for years when dried and are more than satisfactory in the contribution they make to the dried bouquet.

To Dry: Eucalyptus may be hung to dry but a softer, more natural appearance is achieved by processing the sprays in glycerin and water, page 90.

PLUME GRASS   (Erianthus ravennae)   Perennial
PAMPAS GRASS
Flowers: Late summer into autumn

The appearance and texture of the whitish plumes of this tall grass must have reminded early Greeks of wool for they named it *Erion, wool,* plus *anthos, flower.* The popular name, Pampas Grass, came centuries later, after Europeans had found the plant growing in the Pampas regions of South America.

Erianthus is hardy as far north as my garden but it seems to be more popular on the West Coast than on the East. It is often grown as a lawn specimen and established plants produce as many as forty to fifty spikes, up to twelve feet tall, that are topped with plumes sometimes two feet in length.

To Dry: Simply cut, and it is ready to arrange!

JAPANESE BAMBOO *(Polygonum sieboldii)*

Perennial

Fruits: October

There are hundreds of species of *Polygonum* but the one in my garden is *Polygonum sieboldii,* a Japanese plant which arrived in the United States late in the nineteenth century. *Polygonum* is ancient Greek for "many joints" which aptly describes this plant's bamboolike appearance. Its species name, *sieboldii,* honors Phillip von Siebold, a German physician who collected the plant in Japan while in the employ of the Dutch East India Trading Company. The plant is fast growing and attains a height of eight feet in six weeks in my garden. It also spreads very rapidly, which leads me to introduce a note of caution to the unwary gardener: *Polygonum sieboldii,* sometimes called Japanese Knotweed, is a beautiful ornamental perennial but it also behaves like a weed. It is best planted in an open area where it has plenty of elbow room to spread without encroaching on other plants. If you wish to enjoy it as a garden specimen plant it in a five-gallon drum, with the bottom removed, to contain the root runners.

In the fall this species produces sprays of minute red fruit which wing out from the joints.

To Dry: Cut sprays immediately as the fruit turns red. Hang the sprays separately to avoid interference and tearing of the fruit.

Japanese Bamboo

EULALIA *(Miscanthus sinensis var. gracillima)*

Perennial grass

Seeds: October

Old-fashioned names and old-fashioned flowers. From the sixteenth century on, plant materials discovered abroad by European botanists were sent home for classification and naming. Often a new discovery would fire the imagination of the public, whereupon the flower sometimes lent its name to babies born during the period of its popularity. *Eulalia,* which means *well spoken of,* is such a name. As the flower—or grass in this case—found itself supplanted by newer discoveries its name was gradually forgotten, except by those who bore it. Grandma's friend, Eulalia, born before the turn of the century, dates the popularity of this graceful grass.

Miscanthus, its newer name, is native to China and is the one plant material recommended for the *Plant It Now, Dry It Later* garden that does not appear to be readily available to the home gardener. It was usually found in early American gardens where it was massed as a circular lawn specimen. My own clump was a donation from an old-fashioned garden.

Miscanthus is among the last of the plant materials to be cut in the garden in the fall, and it may be used in fresh, as well as dried, bouquets. The renewed demand for this interesting grass may help to increase its availability.

To Dry: Cut in the fall when the seed achenes are fully formed and stand, dry, in a vase. Overnight the sprays of tight achenes burst into graceful, sable-toned, fluffy fountainheads. Arrange alone in a tall narrow-necked vase or with Bittersweet, Chrysanthemums, or other flowers of your choice.

HARDY CYCLAMEN *(Cyclamen neapolitanum)*
Perennial

Flowers: September, October

The gorgeous Cyclamen from the local florist's *(Cyclamen persicum)* does not survive the cold of winter in my northern New Jersey garden, but its cousin *(Cyclamen neapolitanum)* does. I heartily recommend this latter autumn-flowering beauty for a shady corner of the garden, or for wildflower cultivation.

This diminutive plant, one of the twenty-six or so members of the *Cyclamen* family, is a native of the area that extends from the Mediterranean to central Europe. The reddish-pink flowers appear on three- to four-inch stems in the fall, and they are followed by beautifully mottled, olive green leaves which provide an attractive ground cover during the winter months. Both flowers and leaves dry beautifully.

To Dry: Nip the stems of both the flower and the leaf near the base of the plant. Dry the flower and its entire stem as for the single flower, page 81. Allow four days for the stem to harden. The leaf may be wired or not; process it, too, as for the single flower. Allow three days.

NEW ENGLAND ASTER *(Aster novae-angliae)*
MICHAELMAS DAISY
STARWORT
Perennial

Flowers: In the fall

With gay abandon Nature sweeps her paintbrush across New England's autumn landscape adding waves of red, blue, and lavender to the fields and roadsides as the Asters burst into bloom. With other rare plants from "the colonies" this beauty made its way to England and the Continent, where it became a favorite of gardeners and horticulturists. As a consequence of its popularity among European horticulturists the American gardener has available to him improved varieties of New England Asters in luscious shades of pinks, lavender, blue, red, and white that must evoke a sigh of envy from our native beauties. The plants, which grow from three to five feet tall, flower best in full sun. Their roots require considerable moisture.

To Dry: Either a single flower or an entire flower cluster may be processed. Wire and dry either as for the single flower, page 81. Allow three days for the single flower, four days for the flower cluster. Sometimes processing produces colors that hybridizers have been unable to achieve, and in the case of the Aster the lavender becomes an unexpectedly clear blue.

BLACK BIRCH *(Betula carpinifolia)* Tree
Fruits: In the fall

There are about thirty-five members of the Birch family in North America; almost all of them are ornamental and useful trees. Their hard wood is used for furniture, for fuel, and in making charcoal.

The only member of the family to be mentioned here is the Black Birch. Of the many useful purposes it serves mine is probably the least important: my Black Birch provides me with sprays of small cones for dried bouquets. A more important product derived from the branches and foliage of this tree is an oil similar to the oil of wintergreen. The bark is used for flavoring, and I remember, as a child, bruising the young growth to enjoy its flavor and aroma.

The Birches are hardy northern trees and are frequently found in forests. The Black Birch grows from Maine to Alabama and west to Ohio's longitude.

To Dry: No processing is required for the Birch cones. Simply cut the branches with their sprays of cones in the fall, remove the leaves if they have not already fallen, and hang until ready to use.

GROUND PINE *(Lycopodium obscurum)* Perennial
Foliage: From my florist in December

There are about 100 members of the genus *Lycopodium*, but the species that seems to be most sought after for Christmas decoration, to the increasing concern of conservationists, is the Ground Pine *(Lycopodium obscurum)*. The plant, whose short, treelike branches are only six to twelve inches tall, is a native of the North Temperate Zone of the western

Gerard's "Lycopodium" or "Wolfe claw mosse"

hemisphere and Japan. My very limited picking of Ground Pine is confined to the dried and dyed branches available from the florist's in December. The genus name, *Lycopodium,* means *wolflike* in Greek, and refers to the appearance of the spikelike leaves that contain the spores of the plant.

To Dry: These dried and dyed branches are often stiff and flat due to packing, but their softness and three-dimensional appearance are easily restored by submerging them in water overnight. Shake free of excess water and stand in Oasis or Styrofoam to dry.

TEASEL (*Dipsacus* spp)   Biennial

Flowers: In the fall in the local florist garden

Gerard's "Garden Teasell"

"The Cardthistle or Teasel is of two sorts, the tame and the wild. The tame Teasel is sown of fullers and clothworkers to serve their purposes, the wild groweth without husbanding itself, and serveth to small purpose."

The reader of Lyte's *Herbal* in 1578 knew the difference between the cultivated and wild Teasel, but it is of little consequence to today's dried flower arranger whether the Teasel is cultivated and its prickles end in the hooks that were useful in teasing the cloth in the sixteenth century, or wild with straight prickles.

Teasel can be found growing along the roadside from early summer, and at the florist, where it is sometimes dyed in bright colors, in the fall.

To Dry: Cut the stems near the base of the plant. Bundle and hang until needed.

PLANT	ANNUAL PERENNIAL SHRUB TREE BULB CORM	TIME OF FLOWERING or FRUITING, or when cut, if foliage	PROCESSING TECHNIQUE: LAZY FLOWERS MORE EFFORT FLOWERS: (1) Single flower (2) Stalks/Sprays of flowers (3) Flower cluster on sturdy stem FOLIAGE	PROCESSING TIME	RESULTS
Dwarf Iris (Iris reticulata)	Perennial	Late March	More Effort (1)	7 days	Excellent, its blue color remains true

Bibliography

Alexander, Edward Johnston, and Carol H. Woodward. *The Flora of the Unicorn Tapestries.* Reprinted from the *Journal of the New York Botanical Garden,* May and June, 1941.

Bailey, L. H. *The Standard Cyclopedia of Horticulture,* Vols. 1, 2, and 3. New York, the Macmillan Company, 1935.

Bartlett, John. *Familiar Quotations,* 11th edition. Boston, Little, Brown and Company, 1940.

The Botanical Cabinet. Various issues. London, from 1817 to 1833.

Cheng Te-k'un. *Jade Flowers and Floral Patterns in Chinese* Decorative Art. The Chinese University of Hong Kong. Reprinted from *The Journal of the Institute* of Chinese Studies, Vol. II, No. 2, September 1969.

Chittenden, Fred J. (ed., 1st ed.), and Patrick M. Synge (ed., 2nd ed.), The Royal Horticultural Society *Dictionary of Gardening.* Oxford, The Clarendon Press, 1956.

Cholmeley, Margaret. *The Lavender Harvest.* The British Travel Association, *Coming Events in Britain,* July 1958.

Coats, Alice M. *Flowers and Their Histories.* New York, Pitman Publishing Corp., 1956

———. *Garden Shrubs and Their Histories.* New York, Dutton, 1965.

———. *The Plant Hunters.* New York, McGraw-Hill Book Company, 1970.

Curtis's Botanical Magazine. Various issues. London, 1787–1837.

Dioscorides, Pedacius. *Greek Herbal.* Illustrated by a Byzantine A.D. 512. Englished by John Goodyer A.D. 1655. Edited and first printed A.D. 1933 by Robert T. Gunther. London and New York, Hafner Publishing Co., 1968.

Dunthorne, Gordon. *Eighteenth-Century Botanical Prints in Color. The Hunt Botanical Catalogue,* Vol. II, part I, pp xxi–xxxi. Pittsburgh, Pennsylvania, the Hunt Botanical Library, 1961.

Ferron, Maurice. *Essai de destruction de la renouee Japonaise Polygonum cuspidatum Sieb. et Zucc.* Extrait de *Phytoprotection,* Vol. 46, No. 3, pages 125–130, October 1965.

Furber, Robert. *Twelve Months of Flowers.* London, 1730.

Gerard, John. *The Herball,* or *Generall Historie of Plantes.* London, 1633.

Gilmour, John Scott Lennox. *Gardening Books of the Eighteenth Century. The Hunt Botanical Catalogue,* Vol. II, part I, pp xxxii–xxxix. Pittsburgh, Pennsylvania, the Hunt Botanical Library, 1961.

Grenier, Charles. *Flore de France* ou *Description des Plantes en France et en Corse,* Vol. 2. Paris, 1848.

Grieve, Mrs. Maud. *A Modern Herball,* Vols. I and II. New York and London, Hafner Publishing Co., 1967.

Hasselquist, Fredrik. *Voyages and Travels in the Levant in the Years 1749–52.* London, 1766.

Hort, Sir Arthur. *Linnaeus and the Naming of Plants.* Blackwoods Magazine, 1931.

Kent, Elizabeth. *Flora Domestica,* or *The Portable Flower-Garden.* London, 1823.

Li, H. L. *The Garden Flowers of China.* New York, the Ronald Press Company, 1959.

Linne, Carl von. *Critica Botanica.* Leyden, 1737. (English translation by Sir Arthur Hort. London, Printed for The Ray Society, 1938).

Lyte, Henry. *A New Herball;* or, *Historie of Plants.* London, 1595.

Marcus, Margaret Fairbanks. *Flower Paintings by the Great Masters.* New York, H. N. Abrams in association with Pocket Books, 1954.

Meehan, Thomas. *The Native Flowers and Ferns of the United States,* Vols. I and II. Boston, L. Prang & Co., 1878.

Parkinson, John. *Theatrum Botanicum.* London, 1640.

Redoute, Pierre Joseph. *Choix des Plus Belles Fleurs.* Paris, 1807.

Rickett, Harold W. *Wild Flowers of the United States,* Vol. I: *The Northeastern States.* Publication of the New York Botanical Garden. New York, McGraw-Hill Book Company, 1966.

————. Vol. 2: *The Southeastern States.* Publication of the New York Botanical Garden. New York, McGraw-Hill Book Company, 1967.

————. Vol. 3: *Texas.* Publication of the New York Botanical Garden. New York, McGraw-Hill Book Company, 1969.

————. Vol. 4: *The Southwestern States.* Publication of the New York Botanical Garden. New York, McGraw-Hill Book Company, 1970.

Robinson, W. (ed.). *Flora and Sylva,* Vol. I. London, 1903.

Roxburgh, William. *Hortus Bengalensis,* or *A Catalogue of the Plants Growing in the Honourable East India Company's Botanic Garden at Calcutta.* Serampore, 1814.

Salinger, Margaretta. *Flowers: The Flower Piece in European Painting.* The New York Metropolitan Museum of Art Bulletin VIII, 1950, pp 253–261.

Sato, Shozo. *The Art of Arranging Flowers.* New York, Harry N. Abrams, Inc.

Singleton, Esther. *The Shakespeare Garden.* New York, the Century Co., 1922.

Small, John Kunkel. *A Monograph of the North American Species of the Genus Polygonum,* Vol. I. Lancaster, Pa., the New Era Print, 1895.

Stearn, William Thomas. *Botanical Gardens and Botanical Literature in the Eighteenth Century. The Hunt Botanical Catalogue,* Vol. II, part I, pp. xliii–cxxii. Pittsburgh, Pennsylvania, the Hunt Botanical Library, 1961.

Van Wijk, H. L. Gerth. *A Dictionary of Plant Names,* Vols. 1 and 2. Published by the Dutch Society of Science at Haarlem. The Hague, Martinus Nijhoff, 1911.

Wilson, Ernest H. *China-Mother of Gardens.* Boston, the Stratford Company, 1929.

Winkelmann-Rhein, Gertrude, *The Paintings and Drawings of Jan "Flower" Bruegel.* New York, Harry N. Abrams, Inc.

Color Plates As They Appear between Pages 108 and 109

Figures in Black-and-White As They Appear in the Text

Index to "How to" Plant It Now, Dry It Later

Index of Plants

Index of People and Places